Rebuilding Catholic Culture

Ryan N. S. Topping

Rebuilding Catholic Culture

How the *Catechism* Can
Shape Our Common Life

SOPHIA INSTITUTE PRESS
Manchester, New Hampshire

Sophia Institute Press
Box 5284, Manchester, NH 03108
1-800-888-9344

www.SophiaInstitute.com

Sophia Institute Press® is a registered trademark of Sophia Institute.

Library of Congress Cataloging-in-Publication Data
Topping, Ryan.
    Rebuilding Catholic culture : how the Catechism can shape
      our common life / Ryan N. S. Topping.
      pages cm.
    Includes bibliographical references and index.
    ISBN 978-1-933184-94-4 (pbk. : alk. paper) 1. Catholic Church.
      Catechismus Ecclesiae Catholicae. 2. Catholic Church—
      Catechisms. 3. Catholic Church—Doctrines. I. Title.
    BX1959.5.T67 2013
    238'.2—dc23

                                     2012047332

First printing

"In its very structure, the *Catechism of the Catholic Church* follows the development of the faith right up to the great themes of daily life. On page after page, we find that what is presented here is no theory, but an encounter with a Person who lives within the Church."

Pope Benedict XVI, Apostolic Letter Porta Fidei, announcing the 2012–2013 Year of Faith

"Just as faith is a principle of understanding, so obedience must be a principle of freedom. You do not deliver yourself into the hands of authority like a man tired of using his initiative, abdicating; or like a sailor happy to find a quiet harbor at last after a stormy passage. On the contrary, you receive from authority the *Duc in altum*. You entrust yourself to it as to a ship leaving port for a glorious voyage and high adventure."

Henri de Lubac, Paradoxes of Faith, p. 25

Contents

Foreword

It grows daily more apparent that the relation between faith and culture is key to any revival of the Church in the Western world. The lack of an in-depth account of culture is the gaping hole in the heart of the Pastoral Constitution of the Second Vatican Council on the Church in the Modern World, just as the failure of the Council fathers to decide on the drafting of a new universal catechism was the Achilles' heel of their wider project: to rejuvenate the Church by a combination of return to the ancient sources, on the one hand, and accommodation to contemporary idiom on the other. Fortunately, the Council was followed by a pope of enormous determination and visionary power. John Paul II was savvy enough to identify the "hole" made by neglect of the Western cultural domain and to begin to do something about filling it. Likewise, he was brave enough to challenge the radical pluralism that, in the name of decentralization, would have no truck with the notion of a comprehensive confession for the entire Church.

In this book Ryan Topping is the beneficiary of both these advances. Centers for analyzing and documenting, as well as publicizing and celebrating, the relation of faith and culture are now a frequent feature of the ecclesial landscape, while the 1992 *Catechism of the Catholic Church* is steadily acquiring in practice the status of indispensable benchmark that it already occupies in theory.

Dr. Topping has had the excellent idea of glossing the principal overall themes of the *Catechism* in its four constituent books (on, respectively, the Creed, the sacraments, the moral life, and the life of prayer) by reference to the debate on the relation of faith and culture to which his book is a notable contribution. I call the idea excellent because, as pastoral experience everywhere shows, it is impossible to insinuate the Catholic Christian account of reality, and its program for human living, without at the same time seeking to deconstruct those features of the contemporary cultural environment which are in various degrees problematic for the reception of the Church's message. The word *problematic* there marks out a portmanteau category, since the attitudes and trends in present-day culture for which a strenuous exercise of the discernment of spirits is prerequisite range from the unhelpful through the inimical to the downright toxic.

To carry out his aim, Ryan Topping has been obliged to paint on the largest possible canvas, but he does so without losing sight of the key affirmations the *Catechism* serves. He ranges widely in philosophy, politics, literature, ethics, and sociology, both to summon up the spirit of late modernity in the West and to locate the Catholic antidote to its malaise. But, with the genius of the born teacher, he is never in any way hard to follow. This book could be called, in fact, journalism turned into art. If a comparison is needed, it could well be to G. K. Chesterton's more considered pieces, for the style often carries the telltale signs of Chestertonian panache. I have in mind, for instance, such aphorisms as "When God is gone, nature is going"; pithy judgments on predecessors such as "Even without goodwill Kant promised peace among men"; compressed definitions such as "Catholic culture refers to that excellence in thought and manner of life which properly accrues to a people, namely, the Church"; telling critiques such as "Our desire for dialogue has largely overwhelmed our desire to debate, and unsurprisingly heresies abound." No one could doubt the Chestertonian character of Ryan's characterization of the modern agnostic: "You will see painted across his shield not the wild symbols of the Celts, not the fleur-de-lis of the Christians, but only a scribbled message in black ink: 'That's your opinion.'" And if certain images are tougher and more austere (more redolent of the Canadian Prairies?), than is customary with the English apologist—as when we read of the "heart, like some lonely wolf, trot[ting] across the vast and barren plains of our nights and days," the overall thrust of the argument of *Renewing Catholic Culture* echoes Chesterton's deepest insights. The contradictory nature of the criticisms lodged against the faith from a variety of directions witnesses to its truth; its capacity to hold together seeming contradictions attests its sanity. Yet Ryan Topping's manner and mind remain very much his own.

Only someone who has not only observed carefully, but read widely, reflected thoroughly, and experienced deeply can produce a book of this stature. It deserves to take its place among the Catholic classics.

Aidan Nichols, OP

Acknowledgments

The following is based on a lecture series on the *Catechism of the Catholic Church* given in full between 2010 and 2012 in Saskatoon, Saskatchewan, and in North Canton, Ohio, and in part, at several other locations in Canada and in the United States. Each chapter follows the eight-part structure of the *Catechism*. The reader should not expect a systematic commentary upon the seven hundred pages of the Church's guidebook for belief; what is offered, rather, is a series of essays upon the *Catechism's* central conclusions with a view to the renewal of Catholic culture.

In preparing this text I have incurred many debts. In the first place, I should like to thank those friends of mine who attended the lectures and joined in with lively commentary, in particular, Dorothy and Dwight Abernathy, the late Peter Burnell, Terie Jusseaume, Pat and Darlene Kelly, various Sidloskis, Michael Siebert, Connal Tanner, and of course, my wife, Anna Topping. I benefited from the encouragement and criticism of early readers of the manuscript, among them, John Liptay, Fr. David Meconi SJ, Michael O'Brien, Jordan Olver, Joseph Pearce, Fr. John Saward, Matthew Siebert, and Tracey Rowland. Fr. Aidan Nichols, OP, was once a teacher of mine, so it is with particular gratitude that I thank him for his foreword. Institutional support was given by St. Thomas More College (Saskatchewan), Walsh University (Ohio), St. Thomas University (New Brunswick), and Thomas More College of the Liberal Arts (New Hampshire). Several individuals and institutions generously provided images for our use. The staff at Sophia Institute Press was exceedingly helpful.

I thank those editors who have allowed me to incorporate essays that saw print in earlier form elsewhere: "Christology and the Renewal of Catholic Culture," in *Journal of the Canadian Chapter of the Fellowship of Catholic Scholars* (Summer–Fall 2009): 64–99; "The Catechism on How Catholics Believe," in *Homiletic and Pastoral Review* (January 2011): 24–30; "The Intellectual Preconditions for the Renewal of Sacred Architecture," in *Journal of the Canadian Chapter of the Fellowship of Catholic Scholars* (Summer–Fall 2011): 9–29; and, "Dante's *Divine Comedy* and Four Lessons in Fundamental Moral Theology," in *Logos: A Journal of Catholic Thought and Culture* 14:4 (Fall 2011): 43–57; "A New Generation of Theologians," in *First Things/On the Square*, September 27, 2011; "Vatican Two and the Renewal of the Parish Liturgy, Parts I and II," in *Catholic Insight* (July/August and September 2012).

This work is dedicated to Sr. Joseph Andrew Bogdanowicz, OP, and *in honorem Reginae familiae.*

Abbreviations

AA   *Apostolicam Actuositatem*, Decree on the Apostolate of Lay People

CCC   *Catechism of the Catholic Church*

CIC   *Codex Iuris Canonici*, Code of Canon Law

CV   *Caritas in Veritate*, Benedict XVI, Encyclical Letter on Social Teaching

DC   *Deus Caritas Est*, Benedict XVI, Encyclical Letter on the Love of God

DI   *Dominus Iesus*, Congregation for the Doctrine of the Faith, Declaration on the Unicity and Salvific Universality of Jesus Christ and the Church

DPP   *Directory on Popular Piety and the Liturgy*, Congregation for Divine Worship and the Discipline of the Sacraments

DV   *Dei Verbum*, Dogmatic Constitution on Divine Revelation

GS   *Gaudium et Spes*, Pastoral Constitution on the Church in the Modern World

FC   *Familiaris Consortio*, John Paul II, Apostolic Exhortation Regarding the Role of the Christian Family in the Modern World

LA   *Letter to Artists*, John Paul II

LG   *Lumen Gentium*, Dogmatic Constitution on
the Church

LRC   *Letter to the Bishops of the Catholic Church Concerning Reception of Holy Communion by the Divorced and Remarried Members of the Faithful*, Congregation of the Doctrine of the Faith

MD   *Mediator Dei*, Pius XII, Encyclical Letter on the
Sacred Liturgy

PC   *Perfectae Caritatis*, Decree on the Renewal of
Religious Life

RN   *Rerum Novarum*, Leo XIII, Encyclical Letter on
the Condition of the Working Classes

SC   *Sacrosanctum Concilium*, Constitution on the
Sacred Liturgy

SD   *Salvifici Doloris*, John Paul II, Apostolic Letter on
the Christian Meaning of Human Suffering

SP   *Summorum Pontificum*, Benedict XVI, *Motu Proprio*
on the Use of the Roman Liturgy Prior to the
Reform of 1970

SR   *Sacramentum Caritatis*, Benedict XVI, Post Synodal
Exhortation on the Eucharist

SS   *Spe Salvi*, Benedict XVI, Encyclical Letter on
Christian Hope

ST   *Summa Theologica*, St. Thomas Aquinas

VQ   *Vicesimus Quintus Annus*, John Paul II, Apostolic
Letter on the Twenty-fifth Anniversary of *Sacrosanctum Concilium*

VS   *Veritatis Splendor*, John Paul II, Encyclical Letter
on the Church's Moral Teaching

The Annunciation, Masolino da Panicale, Italian, c. 1423, tempera on panel

Introduction

Culture and the Catholic Vision

Have we grown too old for catechisms? Some say so. Even prior to its 1994 English-language publication the *Catechism of the Catholic Church* was greeted by a wall of opposition. Critics said that a definitive guide to faith and morals could never again be achieved. The modern world confesses too many uncertainties; pluralism exposes too many points of view, they said.[1] A catechism is after all an instruction in the faith by question and answer. It is a book of definitions, of certainties, of closures. Question: Who made us? *Answer*: God made us. Question: Who is God? *Answer*: God is the Supreme Being. Question: Why did God make us? *Answer*: God made us to show forth His goodness and to share with us His everlasting happiness in Heaven. The old *Baltimore Catechism* ran through those questions like

---

[1] Extensive documentation of the early and highly critical responses to the *Catechism* can be found in J. Wrenn and K.D. Whitehead's *Flawed Expectations: The Reception of the Catechism of the Catholic Church* (San Francisco: Ignatius Press, 1996); for a brief account of the genesis, structure, and authority of the *Catechism* see Joseph Cardinal Ratzinger and Christoph Schönborn, *Introduction to the Catechism of the Catholic Church* (San Francisco: Ignatius Press, 1994).

a bowling ball, knocking down the riddles of poets and philosophers like sticks, leaving to stand only the skeptic and the half-believer. And they wonder: What kind of game do religious people think they are playing? Bertrand Russell, the twentieth-century British atheist philosopher, once said that it was precisely for this reason that a believer could not produce original intellectual work. Believers presume they already possess answers. So in Russell's *History of Western Philosophy* poor old Thomas Aquinas did not even make the roster in Russell's line-up of greats from Plato to Whitehead. "There is little of the true philosophic spirit in Aquinas," Russell concludes, since as a believer Aquinas can always "fall back on revelation." Apparently, faith is not compatible with all forms of free thinking.[2]

Bertrand Russell was on to something. Faith does impart to our freedom a distinct form. The heart and mind illumined by love no longer act the same, feel the same, think the same. We might even say that religion, once planted and left to go to seed, tends to take over the whole of the garden of the imagination. As T. S. Eliot observed in his *Notes Towards the Definition of Culture*, "There is an aspect in which we see a religion as the *whole way of life* of a people."[3] Like the outside of your window on the morning after winter's first snow, nothing looks quite the same; the world sparkles. That old bench still sits out front, but now it crouches under a white blanket; the trees still stand erect, but now they have become Christmas trees. The world has been made anew.

[2] A *History of Western Philosophy* (New York: Simon and Schuster, 1945), 463.
[3] T. S. Eliot, *Notes Toward the Definition of Culture* in *Christianity and Culture* (New York: Harcourt, Brace and World, Inc., 1949), 103.

Introduction

Iffley Village Lock, Oxfordshire, United Kingdom

Revelation is like that first snow. It is a gift from above. It does not destroy the place beneath, but neither does it leave the earth as it was. Culture is born of our response to revelation. We shape culture, and it in turn shapes us. Like Athena leaping from the head of Zeus, or Mary's bow before the angel, culture follows cult. At the head of Western culture, in ancient Greece, culture quite literally was born from the gods. All the arts (poetry, dance, music, history, etc.) were, in their view, the inspirations of the Muses — those nine sisters within the pantheon who are protectresses of the arts and sciences. Religion was decisive in the formation of Europe too. Cyril and Methodius set out to preach the gospel to the Slavs in A.D. 863, only to find that before they could read them the Bible they had to invent for them a script — the Cyrillic alphabet. In the Middle Ages, we could point to the foundation of the universities in the twelfth century, at Paris, Bologna, and Oxford; or to the birth of hospitals in France in the fourteenth century; or to the rise of the scientific revolution in the seventeenth century. Here, in the New World, we might name Fr. McGivney's development of life-insurance for families in the nineteenth century, or the credit union movement in the twentieth century. Each one of these is an instance of the ongoing transformation of culture by the faith. Wherever you look in the development of Western civilization, and the same could be said of other civilizations, religion is present. It is good that it is here. *Pace* Russell, *pace* Richard Dawkins, once the faith took root in the West its effect was not like a weed where soil is robbed and light choked, but as a lilac tree, emitting a fragrance, an atmosphere within which culture has flourished.

The Catholic claim is that faith makes you truly human: nobler, more just, lovelier than you could have been otherwise. And not only you and me. Nations likewise are elevated by their contact with this living creed. The Faith defines and so limits thought through its dogmas, its institutions, its traditions, but by these the Faith also liberates. By imposing limits faith frees thought and action from futility and can render them divine. In the following chapters I aim to explore and defend that claim.

A definition is in order. The gospel aims to transform culture; but what do we mean by "a whole way of life"? *Culture* derives from the Latin *cultura*, a cultivating, or tilling of the ground. Figuratively *cultura* applied also to the cultivation or improvement of the mind. Thus, in a now slightly older English usage, we call a liberally educated man or woman *cultured*. This mixing of human nature with a tradition of nurture is what produces civilization. But civilization is not the same everywhere. Connected to this is the second sense of our term. *Culture*, borrowing now from the German *Kultur*, can also denote a more

Introduction

The Dancing Couple, Jan Steen, Dutch, 1663

localized pattern of living. We are not born anywhere, but only somewhere. So also the rational and the universal must be given concrete form in particular places. It is this sense of culture that usually denotes the habits of dress, dance, dining, and dying.[4]

[4] Invoking *culture* in this second sense is not without its hazards. Since the end of the nineteenth century English usage has drawn more from the Germanic rather than its Latin roots. In Germany *Kultur* often implies an enclosed system of ideas and habits protected and regulated according to race or language or state government (*Bildung* is the word for "culture" as education). Thus, a temptation today is to speak of one "culture" as incommensurable to another. There is Russian-culture, Afro-American culture, Saudi-culture and, on the dominant sociological interpretation at least, each is immune from criticism that might come from the outside. For background see Tracey Rowland's *Culture and the Thomist Tradition After Vatican II* (London: Routledge, 2003), Christopher Dawson's *The Crisis of Western Education* (Washington, DC, [1961] 2010), 112–115,

Rebuilding Catholic Culture

By speaking of the renewal of Catholic culture I wish to evoke both the universal and particular senses of the term. We can pray for Catholic renewal everywhere; but all good work begins at home. Thus, *Catholic culture* refers to that excellence in thought and manner of life which properly accrues to a people, namely, the Church. The center is the celebration of the Mass. Swirling out from this is a way of life elevated and ennobled by the gospel, touching, as it must, upon the artistic, economic, philosophical, and communal dimensions of existence. At the same time, a culture so defined can take on distinctive forms. Catholic thought and piety will surely not look the same in America as in Armenia; that our Lady appeared at Guadalupe takes nothing away from the devotion that Europeans give to her at Lourdes. Every nation can contribute distinctively to this universal human culture; none can flourish apart from it.

For a generation already, Christians in the developed nations have lived amid the rubble of a ruined culture. The long litany of indicators—the collapse of religious life, vanishing church attendance, banal liturgies, abortion—are familiar enough on our horizon. We in the North Atlantic nations marvel at the fantastic growth in the South. Missionary priests now come to us. We wonder how this happened. Whatever the causes of this decline, what Catholics in Western nations most lack is not goodwill; nor have we—until recent days—lacked political freedom or money. What we lack is confidence. We lack confidence in the world-transforming character of our creed; we lack confidence in the potency of the Faith to shape and redefine the culture of an aggressive modernity that confronts it.

---

and John Burnet's astute lecture "Kultur" in *Essays and Addresses* (London: Chatto and Windus, 1929).

Introduction

There was a prejudice among sociologists in the 1970s and 1980s called the Secularization Thesis, which ran that as modernity advanced, religion would recede. This is, of course, untrue. The rise of global Islam, five hundred million charismatic Christians in the South, the explosion of African and Asian Catholicism, and even the stubborn persistence of belief in the developed world, has buried the idea. Religion remains. Yet, the sociologists were correct in this sense. They were right to see that religion has not been left unscathed. There has been a true clash. The terms of peace between traditional patterns of life and an ever-expanding modernity are conditional. Where the culture of modernity advances unchecked—a culture that we can sum up as progressive, secular, and pluralistic—religion survives in stunted form, taking on one of two roles: therapy or critique. As therapy, religion recedes into the private, offering itself as a coping mechanism. In this mode religion remains as one product among a list of competing remedies that the global consumer digests as required, an occasional sedative for a good night's sleep. As critique, religion occupies a place of discontent, assuming now the role of permanent heresy.[5] Its survival at the margins is even necessary for the justification of the liberal state: religion remains as a trophy to modernity's own universality, its own benign tolerance. Even the Chinese government helps restore an old church now and again.

The following meditations proceed from two assumptions. First, the Church is and remains obliged to make the reign of Christ the King present in every aspect of human life—the school, the concert hall, the legislature, the lab, the home,

---

[5] Slavoj Zizek, *The Puppet and the Dwarf: The Perverse Core of Christianity* (Cambridge, Massachusetts: MIT Press, 2003), 3.

and the mall. Where modernity pretends to offer a creed more universal than the Church's, whether this be through the language of rights, of tolerance, or of inevitable progress, those pretensions need to be exposed; they need to be ridiculed for the idolatry that they are. The Church has a bridegroom who is a jealous lover. The second assumption is this: if Catholicism is ever again to shape Western culture, then the Church in the West must learn anew how to master and muster the resources of its own tradition. This will be done not through endless accommodation to contemporary thought, but through renewal and recovery of its own mind. And in those parts of Western culture where the Church is making advances, this is what she has done. No other institution has been thinking about thinking as long as the Church has. Intellectual humility is a great good, but self-imposed humiliation before our medical, moral, and political masters is unbecoming.

Renewal is a work of the Spirit. It also demands sacrifice. When Fr. Miguel Augustin Pro, the Mexican Jesuit martyr, stretched out his arms before the firing squad on November 22, 1927 he did not proclaim in vain *"Viva Cristo Rey!"* ("Long live Christ the King!"). For Christ is not simply our Good Shepherd; He is also the King. Only the most prosaic and Gnostic versions of the faith could accept as a *fait accompli* the de-centering of religion from public life. Scripture says, "The Son of God came so that we might become partakers of the divine life" (2 Peter 1:4; CCC 460); that principle holds true for our common life as well. As the book of Revelation tells, not only will individuals add their gifts to the glory of the Heavenly City; so too will nations "come bringing their treasure and their wealth" (Rev. 21:26). Among the tasks required for our time, then, is the recovery of the Church's tradition as this is embedded in her

Introduction

creed, in her liturgy, in her moral philosophy, and in her mystical practice. Only then will the *symbols* (liturgical, architectural, artistic), the *language* (of literature and philosophy), and the *confidence* (in matters of faith and morals) of Catholicism enable the Church to succeed in her world-shaping ambition.

A word about the title and structure of this essay. Pope John Paul II once explained, "The body, and it alone, is capable of making visible what is invisible: the spiritual and the divine" (General Audience, February 20, 1980). The resurrection of Lazarus, for instance, did not mark the end of history; what the rising of this dead man's body made tangible was the power of God at work in a new age. Christ raised Lazarus to evoke faith. Christian culture can evoke hope. So I draw an analogy. As in the raising of Lazarus, the renewal of the body of human culture can make present goods that might otherwise remain inaccessible. A vibrant Catholic culture makes intelligible a mode of life and the habits of being that fit us for Heaven. With the end of this renewal in view, there exists no better concise presentation of the Faith than the recently promulgated *Catechism of the Catholic Church*. That text aims "at presenting an organic synthesis of the essential and fundamental contents of Catholic doctrine" (CCC 11) and will provide the basis of our reflections. Its four parts—Creed, Sacraments, Morality, Prayer—comprised two divisions each, making a total of eight sections. The plan is to present key themes in the *Catechism* with reference to the renewal of Catholic culture and that with a view to those challenges that would undermine it. By following the structure, themes, and conclusions of each section of the *Catechism*, and by relating them to dominant philosophical currents, these chapters hope to convey something of that integrated whole of the Catholic vision.

Rebuilding Catholic Culture

The Raising of Lazarus, Benozzo Gozzoli, Italian, c. 1495, oil on canvas

On Faith:
How Catholics Believe

Everyone has seen people gambling with their lives. Sometimes it looks comical, and sometimes it looks sensible; but however it looks, I believe we can learn a lot from watching closely the kinds of risks people regularly take. People do things such as walk onto an airplane, or lie down beneath a surgeon's knife, or throw seeds onto the cold dirt or themselves into the warm arms of a lover. All of these activities rely upon one person trusting another without guarantee that their risk will be rewarded. People do remarkable things like this every day, rich people as well as poor, clever as well as silly.

What interests me about all these activities is that the ordinary man who embarks on such adventures does so not because he despises his life, but because he loves it or, at least, he loves the things that he hopes to accomplish with his life. The farmer tosses seed onto the ground because he hopes it will pop up again, just as much as the man of business steps onto the airplane because he hopes it will bring him down safely again. Everyone knows that sometimes engines fail and seeds rot; but these facts hardly keep businessmen at home or farmers in bed. Vitality, adventure, and gain always include risk. It looks as if the sane passenger, the sane patient, the sane farmer, and the sane lover must act, in order to succeed, according to some virtue or principle of common sense that allows them to function in the way that they do. Now, this principle, what we might call the principle of reasonable trust, is the foundation of personal sanity and of every possible society. The Trust Principle, as we shall name it, may be formulated thus: *trust is a necessary human virtue*. It is necessary because without it we cannot know all the things we need to understand; it is a virtue because trust allows us to do things we could not accomplish on our own.

Some might object: not all people are worthy of trust. We do not always share secrets with our boss, with telemarketers, with the drunkard on the street. This is true, but such examples do not prove a lack of confidence in our principle. Rather, they illustrate it. We appeal to the Trust Principle *especially* when we withhold our trust. When we debate who or what ought to be trusted, it is not the idea of trust that we question; rather, we doubt whether trust is warranted in this or that particular case. When a farmer questions his supplier over whether he should plant chickpeas or wheat, he is unsure not whether plants grow but whether these seeds will survive in his wet soil. When a father questions his daughter as to whether she should marry Robert, it is likely because he doubts not the idea of marriage but the good character of her suitor. In other words, the real question is not whether we believe in the Trust Principle but under what conditions it ought to be invoked.

What are its optimal conditions? There is no general answer. Knowing when and when not to trust someone or something is a matter of prudential judgment. The reasonable person gets on the plane (after, perhaps, he has seen a hundred of them take off and land); the unreasonable person thinks that each smiling stewardess conceals a hidden plot. The reasonable man follows his love to the altar (after, of course, he has made a thorough study of his future in-laws); the unreasonable man never puts on a tuxedo because some women are unfaithful. It seems that strength of action requires a cultivated neglect of thought. The sane man probes, questions, considers, and then flings himself over the rail of unknowing. The reasonable man is reasonable precisely insofar as he knows when deliberation ought to give way to decision and decision over to deed.

The sick man cannot leave his house. The pathological man will not leave his head. Health of mind requires that men do not regard the thousand uncertainties that stand between them and their own front door. When Shakespeare said, "Cowards die many times before their deaths;/The valiant never taste of death but once," he meant that since a man can meet his end only one time, he ought not to be consumed with worry all the time.[6] Bravery is really the most logical disposition. The coward turns out, in the end, not to understand his own self-interests well at all.

None of this is in the least an argument against reason. It is only an argument for the reasonableness of calculated risks. The reasonable person is able to confide in another person even when his knowledge of that person is not exhaustive (could it ever be?). We might say that reasonable trust is more rational than dogmatic disbelief. In the conduct of our daily affairs the Trust Principle seems to be a universal rule of thumb. We simply cannot get along in life without acting on partial knowledge.[7]

---

[6] Shakespeare, *Julius Caesar*, Act II, sc. 2, l. 32–33.
[7] There is an analogous principle at work in the realm of thought. Even though in logic not everything can be proven, it does not follow that logic is illogical. All conclusions come from premises, and premises eventually rest upon axioms. Axioms are

The argument so far has been that sanity involves us in a game of risk. A healthy pagan can recognize this. It is only unhealthy moderns who wish to deny it. If we are going to immerse ourselves in a way of life and thought mapped out by the *Catechism*, courage will be our first duty. To get on with reasoning well, we have to know when reasoning should better well come to an end, when thought must harden into action.

Grasping the truth of the Trust Principle is also to recognize the first step in the argument for faith. The rational man realizes that, by his independent reasoning, he cannot know everything he needs to know so as to flourish. This holds true for great and small matters alike. If we think again of the example of getting onto an airplane, few are likely to verify all the mathematical calculations that went into the design, say, of the six million component parts that a Boeing 747-400 comprises. A sane person is not likely to do this, even though he recognizes that it *might* be done. It is likewise with religion. Most of its claims you can verify by reason and experience; although it is unlikely you ever will. It is unlikely because you would have to master all the languages, absorb all the philosophers, and perfect all of the spiritual disciplines. Most of us never travel that far; yet already in this life we need to get flying. And that is what faith allows us to do. Instead of sitting on the tarmac counting nuts and bolts all your dreary days, faith allows you to get onto the airplane. God gave revelation, then, not to stifle reason, but

---

self-evident truths. The most basic of these is the law of non-contradiction (that a thing cannot both be true and not be true in the same sense in the same place at the same time). To argue against this axiom would be to invoke it; and those who refuse to admit it reduce themselves, as Aristotle says, either to silence or to the status of plants (*Met.*, 1008b).

to let it breathe, to let it grow and give it room to move. Faith offers to reason important material for consideration. It inspires reason to hope that its efforts will be rewarded. This is one reason the Church has always been the greatest patron of learning and the arts and why, when religion fails, so does culture. As G.K. Chesterton once quipped, insofar as religion is gone, reason is going.[8] In sum, we know our reasoning has hit its limit (at least for the time being) when we discover a trustworthy person without whom we cannot get along. In love, this is your spouse; in travel, this is your pilot; in sickness, this is your doctor, or maybe even your priest.

If we are to witness a renewal of Catholic culture, if reason and the arts are to be allowed once more to soar, we will need to be clear about what faith is and what its authorities are. For all of the Michelangelos and the Palestrinas, for all the makers of the English Gothic spires, the French tapestries, and the Italian monasteries, for all the African missionaries and North American martyrs, for all the founders of the new movements and religious houses, for all the faithful living and dead, although scattered across nations and centuries, each holds in common, bound as by a golden thread, the creed of the *Catechism*, the faith of the *unum sanctam Catholicam et Apostolicam Ecclesiam*.

The nature of faith

The following is the *Catechism's* most succinct definition of faith, which will also serve as our point of departure: "Faith is a personal adherence of the whole man to God who reveals himself. It involves an assent of the intellect and will to the self-revelation God has made through his deeds and words" (CCC

---

[8] G.K. Chesterton, *Orthodoxy* (San Francisco: Ignatius Press, 1995), 39.

176). St. Augustine (354–430) recognized that we use the word *faith* for both a set of beliefs (*fides quae*) and the virtue that enables us to hold those beliefs (*fides qua*).[9] The two operations correspond to the intellectual and volitional aspects of faith to which the *Catechism* makes reference.[10]

This early distinction that found its way into the *Catechism* is present in the Bible, particularly in the writings of the apostles Paul and John. In the New Testament we find two basic images of faith that provide a framework for all later thinking on the subject. The first is the Pauline account. Here faith (*pistis*) is willed trust in that which you cannot prove. In the letter to the Romans Abraham is held up as a model of faith. Righteousness was reckoned to Abraham because, despite his age and Sarah's barrenness, "he hoped and believed that he was to become the father of many nations in fulfillment of the promise" (Rom. 4:18). Similarly, the letter to the Hebrews presents a similar image: "Faith is the assurance of things hoped for, the *conviction* of things not seen" (Heb. 11:1). This is what we might call the affective or volitional aspect of faith. We have *faith* (*pistis*)

---

[9] As he writes in *De Trinitate* 3.15: "We say truly that faith has indeed been impressed from out of one doctrine upon the hearts of each believer who believes this same thing. But those things which are believed (*quae creduntur*) are one thing, the faith by which they are believed (*fides qua creduntur*) another" (*Ex una sane doctrina impressam fidem credentium cordibus singulorum qui hoc idem credunt uerissime dicimus, sed aliud sunt ea quae creduntur, aliud fides qua creduntur*).

[10] See further Aidan Nichols, *The Shape of Catholic Theology: An Introduction to Its Sources, Principles, and History* (Collegeville, Minnesota: The Liturgical Press, 1991), 13–26; and texts and copious notes in the English Dominican edition of St. Thomas's *Summa Theologica*, vol. 31: Faith, ed. T.C. O'Brien (London: Blackfriars, 1974).

The Knight of Men, Master E.S., German, 1463, engraving

in God in a way similar to the way we have *trust* in the word of an old friend. Past deeds build confidence in future promises. This is one reason marriage and the military have always been esteemed in Christian societies. These two institutions are built upon the virtue of honor, of keeping faith. Faithfulness in people helps to make God more believable. Faithfulness is the leading virtue of Chaucer's Knight in the *Canterbury Tales*, who loved "chivalrye, Trouthe, and honour, freedom and curteisye" (Prologue, l.45). Become trustworthy, and you become a living image — literally an icon — of God (Gen. 1:27). Fidelity in marriage is the cultivation of faith as *willed trust,* which the letter to the Hebrews develops.[11]

[11] In the Protestant Reformation Martin Luther emphasized this first aspect of faith, most persuasively in his *On the Freedom*

While faith is certainly trust in God, it is not only trust in God. The second image of faith in the New Testament is found in St. John's writings. John treats faith more as the first stage of illumination, an incipient understanding. For instance, in John's Gospel, Jesus pleads with the Jews who cannot yet accept him to open their eyes to the evidence they can see: "Believe the works, so that you may know and understand" (John 10:38). Here faith is a stage along one's way. It is incomplete sight. It is the first meeting with a college roommate. At the end of your university years you look back on that meeting and marvel: you recognize that the friend you know now is the same person you met two or twenty years ago, but how much more of him you understand!

So faith or belief (*pistis*) has both a volitional and an intellectual aspect to it. Because of faith we believe things we couldn't have imagined on our own; by faith we accomplish things that we would never have done otherwise. In the next chapter we shall address directly the place of reason in the life of faith, but here I wish to point out two further conditions for faith: a set of subjective conditions and a set of objective ones. The subjective conditions are the psychological dispositions or virtues that make the soul receptive to the gift of faith; the objective conditions for faith are the external conditions that must be present if such a submission of intellect and will is to be rationally justified.

Faith on the inside

I take first the subjective correlates. Mystics and theologians stress how even the intellectual aspect of the act of faith

---

of a Christian (1520); through the success of Evangelicalism it is also the part of faith with which many Christians are most familiar. See further B. A. Gerrish, *Grace and Reason: A Study in the Theology of Luther* (Oxford: Clarendon Press, 1962).

is not solely a matter of the intellect. Seeing by faith requires purity of heart. There are psychological conditions that must be met. This is why the Greek father Evagrius Ponticus says in his fourth-century manual *On Prayer* that the true theologian is the one who prays (*On Prayer* §61). Theology is, according to its most enduring definition given first by St. Augustine, *fides quaerens intellectum*, faith seeking understanding (cf. *Epistle* 120). Faith is intellectual; it is never merely academic. Without purity of heart, the intelligence remains closed to God. Enlightenment requires conversion.

An ancient Greek proverb ran, "Like is known by like"; a modern equivalent might be, "It takes one to know one." For the intellectual life, this means that you must love first before you can learn. This condition of soul is demanded as much from the good novelist as from the good physicist, the good teacher as much as the good police officer. Human nature, atoms, children, and justice are all loved by those who serve them well. It is no different with God. In theology this likeness between subject and object has a technical term, *connaturality*. In his masterpiece in moral theology, *Veritatis Splendor*, John Paul II explained the subjective requirements of theology this way:

> What is essential is a sort of *"connaturality" between man and the true good.* Such a connaturality is rooted in and develops through the virtuous attitudes of the individual himself: prudence and the other cardinal virtues, and even before these the theological virtues of faith, hope and charity. This is the meaning of Jesus' saying: "He who does what is true comes to the light" (*Jn* 3:21). (VS 64)

He who does what is true comes to the light: to become like God is to be connatural with him. So, unlike the modern reductionist view in which the knowing subject can remain distant and aloof from its object, in the classical and Christian view, all learning, but especially theology, requires transformation. Winning intimacy with God is like winning any beloved: you must become worthy to share in their secrets.

But is faith itself a secret? The *Catechism* is clear that the theological virtue of faith is a gift. God initiates his contact with man by revelation, and God provides for man "the grace of being able to welcome this revelation in faith" (CCC 35). It would be wrong to conclude from the above, however, that reason is simply dumb before the mystery.

Indeed, since the First Vatican Council (1870) it has been a point of dogma that reason can, of its own, firmly establish God's existence. Recognizing the value of these proofs (from motion, from contingency, from conscience, etc.),[12] which philosophers from nearly every age have acknowledged as sound, is crucial for the coherence of theology. Structurally, the fact that we can demonstrate religion's first principles keeps faith from spinning off into wild fideism or dull superstition.[13] Even more, the natural use of reason can "predispose one to faith" (CCC 35).

So, faith is a gift of God. It is a gift that extends our rational capacities, not one that simply bypasses them altogether. We can, to a limited extent, even prepare ourselves for faith. As Simone Weil (1909–1943), a Jewish philosopher and near convert, once wrote of Christ: "If one turns aside from him to

---

[12] Peter Kreeft and Fr. Ronald Tacelli nicely summarize twenty of them in their *Handbook of Catholic Apologetics* (San Francisco: Ignatius Press, 2009).

[13] On this see further Aquinas's *Exposition of Boethius' On the Trinity*, Q. 2. art. 3.

go toward the truth, one will not go far before falling into his arms."[14]

Understanding what Catholics mean by *faith* requires that we put aside at least one common prejudice: that scientific proofs are the only means by which the mind can attain knowledge. Since the eighteenth century we moderns have tended to reduce knowledge to the conclusions of experimental science. What we can touch can be measured; what we can measure we can know. Too often all else is relegated to opinion. Because of this philosophical legacy we habitually divide the world into separated compartments, facts and values. Science gives us knowledge about the world, while religion, morality, and art trade in that badly inflated currency of "values." The problem is not that we ignore values but that we give them too much attention and forget what they replaced in our moral taxonomy. Values as *willed* meanings replaced the more sturdy language of good and evil.

The early modern tunneling of reason's vision into the world that can be squeezed under a microscope has, of course, long come under scrutiny in academic circles. But in the popular imagination informed by the *Globe and Mail* or the *New York Times*, and those who generally police our public life, it has not. A recent case will serve to illustrate. In 2010 it was announced that the Canadian Association of University Teachers (CAUT) had in late 2009 launched an "investigation" into the academic integrity of Trinity Western University, Langley, British Columbia. As might be inferred from its name, Trinity Western is a Christian university. Embedded within its institutional ethos is a commitment to certain non-negotiable claims about reality.

[14] Simone Weil, *Waiting for God* (London: Routledge Kegan Paul, 1951), 36.

Faculty members must personally declare their belief that God exists, that Jesus is the Christ, and several other such articles generally held by Christians. Although the organization had received no complaints about the university, CAUT considered the learning and teaching environment of the institution compromised. Of course, work at the institution is voluntary, and its funding largely private, but for CAUT, this is all too restrictive. The association has been pressuring Trinity Western to drop its requirement that faculty sign a statement of faith. As CAUT explained, it wishes the university can bring itself into line with the standard of academic freedom that, well, secular universities enjoy.[15]

What are we to make of this? Anyone who has spent more than a week in a Canadian or American public university with

[15] In response to criticisms, CAUT has consistently declared that its actions against Trinity Western, Canadian Mennonite University (Winnipeg, Manitoba), and also Redeemer Baptist University (Halifax, Nova Scotia) betray no anti-Christian bias, but simply the desire to uphold the principle of academic freedom wherever a threat is perceived. One wonders if they are in jest. Some measure of the organization's nerve can be gauged by the advice they recently offered to St. Mary's University in Halifax, Nova Scotia, when Professor Peter March did experience genuine threats to his freedom. In February 2006 Dr. March posted on his door the cartoons depicting Mohammad first published in the Danish newspaper Jyllands-Posten. When Muslim students discovered this, about one hundred students made a public demonstration in opposition. Some apparently threatened to firebomb the institution should the posters remain. The administration asked Dr. March to take the posters down; when he refused, the administration asked CAUT to advise whether ordering Dr. March to remove the images would violate his academic freedom. In reply CAUT recommended the images be taken down "on health and safety grounds."

their eyes open could hand you a list of dogmas that you are not free to question. (Ever met a professor of Women's Studies who took issue with feminism?) The notion of *absolute* academic freedom is fantasy. Even in the natural sciences there are obvious institutional pressures to conform your research to the fads of the day, to what is amenable to your departmental supervisor, and most of all to what funding agencies expect. Secular universities have their dogmas too. And dogma number one is that you can never prove things that you cannot see. A dizzying diversity of opinion exists at most universities. Unfortunately this is a diversity increasingly founded upon a dull, homogeneous skepticism. Inside the secular university the rule of thumb is this: you may take religion or leave it as you like, as long as you do not take it seriously.

Faith builds upon reason. It requires a willingness to believe in reasonable authorities. Eliminate trust, eliminate the idea of confidence in persons, and you eliminate the very possibility of travel, of medicine, of education, or love and a heap of other good things that brighten our days with joy. If you are a sane man, what you have to figure out is not whether you should trust other people, for that seems necessary, but whether *this* risk is reasonable or *that* person is trustworthy. In what does the Catholic Church ask us to put our trust?

Faith on the outside

Catholicism claims to be a revealed religion and a total system of life. Faith requires receptivity to God and purity of heart. Faith requires also an exterior pattern, an objective form that gives shape to our assent. According to the Church, revelation is that form which God's self-disclosure takes, and it has three sources: Scripture, Tradition, and the Magisterium. Since we shall appeal to these in the following chapters, some discussion of them now would be helpful. Of the first authority all Christians agree; of the second, Catholics and Orthodox are in close union; the third belongs distinctively to Papists.

St. Jerome once said that ignorance of the Scriptures is ignorance of Christ (*Commentariorum in Isaiam libri*, xviii prol.; CCC 133). The *Catechism* relates that, for Catholics, "Sacred Scripture is the speech of God as it is put down in writing under the breath of the Holy Spirit" (CCC 81). The word *Bible, biblos* in Greek, simply means "the Book." The Bible is the book of books—a title reflecting the ancient Jewish belief that God spoke through the written word. Of itself, the Bible testifies: "All Scripture is inspired by God" (cf. 2 Tim. 3:16; cf. 2 Macc. 2:13, Rom. 1:2).

As a Jew, Jesus highly venerated the Scriptures. When a boy, Christ questioned the teachers of the law in the Temple; as a man, he read in the synagogue; while a preacher, he promised that not one word of it shall pass away. Following from this model, early Christians also revered the Scriptures, often guarding them with their lives. Unlike some forms of Protestantism, however, the Church has never forgotten the mystical nature of the Book and the variety of keys required to unlock her secrets.

There are four senses of the text that need to be kept in view. The medieval couplet ran, "Littera gesta docet, quid credas allegoria, moralis quid agas, quo tendas anagogia" (CCC 118):

> *The Letter speaks of deeds;*
> *Allegory to our faith;*
> *The Moral, what we ought to do*
> *Anagogy, to our resting place.*

Thus the story of the great flood recounts a literal event. But more importantly, as St. Augustine says, it informs the

Noah's Ark, Jacques Callot, French, c. 1635, etching

reader that the Church of God is the ark of salvation (allegory), admonishes Christians to seek true doctrine within the
Church (moral), and reassures all that the Church's journey
through time—this is the highest mystical significance of the
story—will transport us to the safety of our heavenly country
(anagogy) (cf. *City of God*, 15.27–28).[16]

In addition to the four senses of Scripture Catholics are
taught to keep in view two further principles of interpretation.
The first is, as it were, a negative guideline: the Bible does not
tell us everything we need to know. Even when you are not limited to literal interpretations of the Bible, you are still limited
to interpretations. "The devil can cite Scripture too," the old

[16] See also Henri du Lubac, *Medieval Exegesis, volume 1: The Four
Senses of Scripture*, trans. M. Sebanc (Grand Rapids, Michigan:
William B. Eerdmans, 1998).

adage goes. And the presence of some thirty-three thousand Protestant denominations — increasing at a rate of 182 per year (i.e., one every two days), according to Barrett's *World Christian Encyclopedia*[17] — is certainly exploited by some as evidence that Luther's *sola scriptura* principle is not without its difficulties. Indeed, the Church existed for decades before the New Testament was written and centuries before the canon was formed. There was never a moment when the text preceded the community from which it sprang. Hence, from the first principle comes a second: Scripture is interpreted best from within the Church. Reading the Gospels of Matthew, Mark, Luke, and John from outside of the unbroken apostolic community robs the written word of its living voice. The Campbells' family photo album makes most sense when you have actually met the Campbells and their children. Likewise, the Bible is better understood when you know the family of whom it speaks. The Church is this family.

The second principle (reading the Bible with the Church) can be explained in philosophical terms as well. No written word can adapt to, argue with, dispute, or even answer the friendly questions its readers might raise. In this respect the Bible is no different from other texts. As opposed to Islam, Christianity is not a religion of the "Book." For Catholics, Scripture contains but does not circumscribe the Word of God. The deficiency of the written word is an old problem raised already in Plato's *Phaedrus*. Words, once set down, lose something of their vitality, of their capacity to address readers. Written words are like the creations of a painter. Although a pre-Raphaelite heroine might dazzle and even overwhelm with its beauty, a young man

---

[17] Oxford, 2001, 2nd ed., 1:10 and 1:5.

Our Lady's children

will kiss only lips that speak. A man needs a living bride. Texts share the same limitations as paintings. Plato makes the point: "You'd think they were speaking as if they had some understanding," but question them and they remain silent. What is more: "When it's attacked unfairly, it always needs its father's support; alone, it can neither defend itself nor come to its own support" (*Phaed.*, 275de).

On the methods of interpretation of the Bible Catholics differ considerably from most Protestant groups. On the interpretation of divine revelation Catholics insist, where Protestants do not, on the mediating significance of the Church, not only of today but as it extends throughout time. We said that the Bible is like a family album. Well, that family has a living history which is what Catholics mean by Tradition. In sum, to read as a

Catholic is to keep a few basic principles in view. Passages can be read in four senses; the Bible is not the whole of revelation; it must be read in the light of tradition. Only read in this way can the Word remain living and active as God intends it. As the Eastern Orthodox theologian Metropolitan Kallistos Ware says, "The final criterion for our interpretation of Scripture is the mind of the Church. And this means keeping constantly in view how the meaning of Scripture is applied in Holy Tradition: that is to say how the Bible is understood by the Fathers and the saints, and how it is used in liturgical worship."[18]

Catholics share the Bible with Protestants, but with the Orthodox they hold a common devotion to Sacred Tradition. How do Scripture and tradition relate?

The *Catechism* subsumes Scripture under the category of tradition. Scripture is "subsumed" not in the sense of being less authoritative than Tradition but as belonging within it. The Bible is the result of a larger mechanism of transmission that Catholics refer to as the Church's Tradition. After all, what has become the New Testament was written, preserved, and declared canonical by the Apostles and their successors, the bishops. From its inception, therefore, the Bible is the product of the Church of Christ. Seen in this light, it is perhaps easier to recognize why in the Catholic view the concept and reality of a living tradition is required to safeguard the authentic interpretation of Scripture. As the *Catechism* puts it: Holy Tradition "transmits in its entirety the Word of God which has been entrusted to the Apostles" (CCC 81). Between Tradition and Scripture there is distinction, but not opposition. Scripture belongs within the ongoing transmission of the Faith. It

---

[18] *The Orthodox Way* (Crestwood, New York: St. Vladimir's Seminary Press, 1990), 147–148.

guides the development of doctrine; it does not end it. *Traditio* (from which we get *tradition*) literally means "that which is handed over." What the Apostles handed on was both an oral and a written teaching that, from the beginning, informed one another. Scripture itself testifies to such a process. We see an example of this when St. Paul in his letter to the Corinthians writes: "The tradition I handed on to you in the first place, a tradition which I had myself received, was that Christ died for our sins" (1 Cor. 15:3). Therefore, in Catholic thought, even if the Bible is a privileged repository within the Tradition, it remains within and not outside of the teachings of the Apostles as they were handed forward. The Bible and Tradition are two expressions of the one Word of God. Of this the *Catechism* concludes:

> As a result the Church, to whom the transmission and interpretation of Revelation is entrusted, "does not derive her certainty about all revealed truth from the holy Scriptures alone. Both Scripture and Tradition must be accepted and honoured with equal sentiments of devotion and reverence." (CCC 82; quoting DV 9)

Before we describe how the Magisterium functions as the third authority or source of revelation, it might be helpful to register an historical aside. The contemporary Catholic view on the relationship between Scripture and Tradition can appear deceptively uncomplicated. It is not. The *Catechism*'s presentation is actually a synthesis of notions developed over the last two councils. To get a clearer view of where Catholics now stand on the relation between Scripture and Tradition, we need to consider the alternative models of that relationship that were rejected. In striking the present balance the *Catechism* reflects the Church's desire to give adequate weight to both the propositional and historical character of revelation.

At the First Vatican Council the Church had to respond to certain problems in philosophy, while the fathers at the Second Vatican Council had to address difficulties in hermeneutics. In 1870 the bishops felt the need to reassert integrity of our natural knowledge of God. Against Kantian philosophy they reaffirmed the propositional character of revelation. By 1962, the mood had changed. Now the fathers had to address the influence of *history*. Even if we grant that God has spoken through Scripture and Tradition, speech is always embedded within particular linguistic and cultural patterns. The Jews had to read the Law in Hebrew; Jesus was born in Roman-occupied Palestine. How much of a prophet's teaching is shaped by his place and time?

Anyone who has attempted to conjugate a foreign verb is aware of the difficulties. A modern Briton will formulate a sentence differently from a German speaker; both think in categories that at times would be alien to an ancient Roman. At the Second Vatican Council the right use of the Bible had become contested as a consequence of two trends in (particularly) Protestant scholarship. The "historical-critical" method, exemplified by figures such as Rudolf Bultmann (1884–1976), emphasized the historical and contingent elements within the Bible. This school explored in detail the common customs that united the writers of the Hebrew Bible to their ancient Near Eastern neighbors. Scholars have made amply clear that not everything the Jews thought about food, about law, or about slavery was unique. To such insights, we might respond: why should we expect the Jews to have been totally unlike the Sumerians and Babylonians? As Pope Benedict XVI has many times reaffirmed, notably in his *Jesus of Nazareth: From the Baptism in the Jordan to the Transfiguration*, this search for connections between the ideas of biblical writers and their surrounding milieu is not problematic in itself. Indeed, for a more complete view of God's work in time, it is essential.

The historical-critical approach can hinder our understanding, however, when scholars lose sight of the method's limits. To the degree that exegetes assume that the reconstruction of a specific biblical writer's circumstance, motivation, and rhetorical strategies—where, why, and how he wrote the text—is not only necessary but *sufficient* to account for what the Bible means, they (falsely) presume what their method cannot justify. St. Luke spoke Greek because he was born a pagan; it may be that his emphasis on women, pregnancy, and the poor can be traced to his training as a physician, but these accidents of personality alone do not account for his Gospel. It does not follow that because ideas have a beginning in one time or place, they are therefore limited to one time or place. Thus, scholars err when they presume that the category of revelation must be subsumed into the matrix of history. As Benedict has written, "The standard for evaluating [Scripture] is not found in merely historical data."[19] Lurking behind the often-held view among exegetes is the assumption (developed in the modern era first by Immanuel Kant) that man never reaches the thing in and of itself.

This presumption is not confined to biblical scholars. In contemporary idiom, when skepticism is embraced, all that remains is discourse, words about words. This is what the French postmodern philosopher Jacques Derrida (1930–2004) meant by his celebration of *différance*. Since, as he claimed, words cannot carry us over into contact with objects, there remains in our

---

[19] Joseph Ratzinger, *On the Way to Jesus Christ* (San Francisco: Ignatius Press, 2005), 92.

language only endless deferral of meaning: words about words about words about words.[20] Discerning what was true and what was false amid the claims advanced by proponents of "scientific study" of the Bible and linguistic analysis was one front the bishops had to face. From the other side of Protestant theology, especially from among its conservative elements, was the charge not that the Church took the Bible too seriously but that Catholics regarded it not seriously enough. The story of Scripture was lost. History, so it appeared, had been silenced by metaphysics. The narrative of God's saving action had been buried under scholastic systems. This claim was put forth most strongly by Karl Barth (1886–1968), whom, apparently, Pope Pius XII said was the most important theologian since Thomas Aquinas.

In relation to these mid-twentieth century trends, the council, and following this the *Catechism*, struck a nuanced balance between Tradition and the Bible, history and metaphysics. On the Bible: Old and New Testaments are a privileged repository of Tradition, to be sure, but they serve as a fixed rudder, not as a chain to port. Scripture sets a trajectory of development. It does not stop the Church from ever setting sail.

"Aha!" we can imagine a Baptist brother exclaim. "Finally I understand how you Catholics justify worship of Mary!" This is a fair response. Why not worship Mary? If Scripture and Tradition are honored "with equal sentiments of devotion" how then do

[20] See Derrida's essay "Différance" (originally published in 1968) in his *Margins of Philosophy*, translated with notes by Alan Bass (Chicago: University of Chicago Press, 1982), in which he concludes, for instance: "One could no longer include *différance* in the concept of the sign, which always has meant the representation of a presence, and has been constituted in a system (thought or language) governed by and moving toward presence" (p. 10).

On Faith

Column of Mary, erected 1638,
Marienplatz, Munich, Germany

we separate the good parts of tradition from the bad? Once the Bible ceases to function as the sole limiting criterion, it becomes less clear what keeps the Church from losing her way. The hermeneutical problem for Catholic and Orthodox Churches is this: like Scripture, Tradition requires interpretation; it appears, however, that there is no universally acknowledged subject in which "Tradition" inheres; therefore it is unclear as to how Tradition can act as a norm of faith. Amid the bulky mass of prayer books, rosaries, theological tracts, witch hunts, crusaders, and mystics, how is the authentic bearer of Tradition identified?

Catholics do well not to dismiss such a conclusion lightly. Theologically, of course, the subject in which Tradition adheres is the Church. But even that requires specification. After all, distinguishing true representatives from pretenders (such as Arius, Donatus, Luther ...) is precisely what appeal to Tradition aims to answer, at least in those moments when its meaning is in dispute. On this point Roman Catholic and Eastern Orthodox Christians find themselves in near but not complete agreement.[21] In the identification of authentic Tradition, the Catholic Church, of course, makes its final appeal to the Magisterium—the teaching office of the bishops in union with the Bishop of Rome.

Of this also we will have more to say in later chapters. For now we note that as an article of faith, Catholics believe that the Pope will never lead the Church into error, at least in his doctrinal formulations of matters of faith and morals. History well attests that popes can be corrupt, inept, and imprudent; but they have never—so Catholics claim—proposed as a matter of belief anything contrary to faith (CCC 890). Besides this, Catholics think there are purely logical reasons for why such a thing as a Magisterium is necessary. For the best account of this one may look to John Henry Cardinal Newman, who in his *Essay on the Development of Doctrine* (1845) argued that if God in fact did communicate a revelation he must also have established some mechanism for its interpretation. As Newman wrote on the eve of his conversion:

> If Christianity is both social and dogmatic, and intended for all ages, it must humanly speaking have an infallible

---

[21] We note that even among themselves, the Orthodox have no unified solution. The last acknowledged ecumenical council is Nicaea II in 878—and, despite efforts over the past one hundred years, they have not been able to organize even a pan-Orthodox council.

expounder. Else you will secure unity of form at the loss of unity of doctrine, or unity of doctrine at the loss of unity of form; you will have to choose between a comprehension of opinions and a resolution into parties, between latitudinarian and sectarian error. [22]

Conclusion

In this opening meditation on the *Catechism* we have attempted to clarify the nature and sources of authority to which Catholics can look in the shaping of Catholic culture. Against those who would deny faith altogether we have suggested that trust is necessary to sanity, and further, that most sane of all would be those who trusted God, should he wish to speak. The Catholic claim, of course, is that God did speak. But that revelation, if it is to be heard, requires both inner conversion and attention to the outer forms of revelation. According to the Catholic *Catechism*, belief demands both renewal of heart and at the same time ever renewed attention to Scripture, to Tradition, and to the Magisterium. If the Church is to reclaim culture as a medium of God's saving work, then living tradition cannot be consigned to the past. It will have to become for us, in our architecture, in our painting, in our music, in our literature, and in our theology once more a living and vital force if we are not to abandon ourselves to the spirit of the age. To add substance to this proposition we turn next to the Creed, and to the Christian's most exalted work, in the Liturgy.

[22] John Henry Cardinal Newman, *An Essay on the Development of Doctrine*, foreword by Ian Ker (Notre Dame, Indiana: University of Notre Dame Press, 1989), 90–91.

The Adoration of the Magi, Fra Angelico,
Italian, c. 1450, tempera on panel

On the Creed:
Why Christology Matters

G. K. Chesterton once quipped that if some small mistake were made in doctrine, huge blunders might be made in human happiness:

> A sentence phrased wrong about the nature of symbolism would have broken all the best statues in Europe. A slip in the definitions might stop all the dances; might wither all the Christmas trees or break all the Easter eggs.[23]

From the inner and outer forms of faith we turn with the *Catechism* to its substance in the Creed. As we read in the *Catechism*, at the center of the Creed is Jesus Christ: "At the heart of Catechesis we find, in essence, a Person ... the Person of Jesus of Nazareth, the only son of the Father" (CCC 426). Catholic culture is ever the fruit of Christian humanism. The polyphony, the poetry, and the soaring cathedrals produced by Christendom are the outgrowths of the novel point of view that because God became man, man can become God. No Christ, no true humanism; no Christ, no Catholic culture. That Catholic culture is in need of renewal need hardly be defended. What

---

[23] Chesterton, *Orthodoxy*, 107.

I wish to highlight here is the distinctive role that Christology plays — and should have played — in the cultural project of transforming all things in Christ. Our question: How might a renewal in Christology help revivify our common life? To help us get this right, it will be useful to look back to see what went wrong, at least over the past forty some years. Our reflections divide unevenly between two parts, a long survey and a brief suggestion. First, a survey of a (failed) attempt to reconcile Christian and secular humanisms; second, a suggestion as to why orthodox religion remains romantic, and even our best hope for guarding joy in an age sunk in sadness.

Christology and anthropology at Vatican II

Many of the damaging trends in Christology over the past forty years took for their justification a specious interpretation of *Guadium et spes*. Out of the desire to enter into dialogue with

St. Peter's Basilica, Rome

"the modern world" much postconciliar thought set aside the council's distinctively christological texts in an effort to high-light convergences between Catholic and secular humanisms. As we know, Vatican II did not in fact signal the beginning of a new religion. Largely because of the efforts of the last two pontificates, the project of reinventing Catholicism from ground zero has now been exhausted, if not in fact at least in theory. Why did the Second Vatican Council initiate a crisis of faith for so many in the Church?

At the heart of the Second Vatican Council was the Pastoral Constitution on the Church in the Modern World (*Gaudium et Spes*), whose core is paragraph 22: "In reality it is only in the mystery of the Word made flesh that the mystery of man truly becomes clear." As has often been observed, the texts of Vatican II seem to provide the basis for a range of readings. There is a reason for this. Unlike the Council of Nicaea in the fourth century, or Trent in the sixteenth, by focusing upon questions of pastoral mission and evangelization, Vatican II provided no obvious key to its own interpretation.

Aggiornamento, updating, was the term many used to capture the spirit of the great event. With some 2,500 bishops and religious superiors from all over the globe, with virtually every aspect of the Church's life on the table, it is not unfair to characterize the council as a singular event in Catholic history. Pope John XXIII said that he wished the Church to open her windows to the modern world. Instead of meeting heresies, of deepening matters of fundamental theology, good Pope John wished his council to be pastoral. Along this line in his opening remarks he addressed the bishops in words that fifty years hence could be taken as unreasonably optimistic. There he suggested that in the past, and in her approach to heretics, the

Church had too often delivered the darts of discipline and too rarely extended the medicine of mercy; unlike the previous twenty ecumenical councils, this one would initiate a dialogue with "the modern world." Nowhere is that ambition fulfilled as directly as in *Gaudium et Spes*.[24]

It seems that no sooner had the council closed than controversy over its meaning opened up. The reception of Paul VI's *Humanae Vitae* was emblematic. When the Eastern Orthodox Ecumenical Patriarch Athenagoras I heard that Paul VI had reaffirmed the Church's unbroken teaching on artificial contraception, the Patriarch congratulated the pontiff, adding that in this matter "we are in total agreement with you."[25] Not everyone claimed to be so. Canadian, Dutch, and German bishops responded that individuals' consciences should rule. With the Canadian Conference of Catholic Bishops' infamous 1968 "Winnipeg Statement," the bishops assured couples that as long as one "honestly chooses" to disregard the moral teaching of the Church on sexual questions, they may do so "in good conscience."[26] In this statement, which has never been

---

[24] Helpful background to the council is found in George Weigel's account in *Witness to Hope: The Biography of Pope John Paul II* (New York: Harper Collins, 2005), 153–155.

[25] After the publication of *Humanae Vitae* the patriarch telegraphed Paul VI, saying: "We assure you that we remain close to you, above all in these recent days when you have taken the good step of publishing the encyclical *Humanae Vitae*. We are in total agreement with you, and wish you all God's help to continue your mission in the world. With much brotherly affection"; reprinted in *Towards the Healing of Schism: The Sees of Rome and Constantinople*, ed. and trans. E. J. Stormon (Mahwah, New Jersey: Paulist Press, 1987), 197.

[26] The Canadian Conference of Bishops' "Winnipeg Statement" offered that couples who dissent from *Humanae Vitae* "should

retracted, the bishops supplied no criteria according to which the faithful should judge when they have chosen "honestly" as opposed to — we must presume — "dishonestly." Nor was there indication as to which other precepts may be disregarded "in good conscience." Few bishops defended Paul VI with vigor. Among academics, theologians in Europe and America began to speak of an "alternative magisterium." For the first time Catholics were introduced to the concept of "loyal dissent."[27] Also in 1968, a young peritus, the Canadian theologian (and then Augustinian priest) Gregory Baum, likewise described the council as "the beginning of the beginning of a profound doctrinal reform." With reference particularly to moral theology, and pointing to *Gaudium et Spes*, Baum offered some indication as to where this reform would likely lead:

> The entire moral teaching of the Church … is inadequate. The present crisis in regard to birth control is just one instance of this inadequacy. None of the official

---

not be considered, or consider themselves, shut off from the body of the faithful" (§17). The document concluded that: "if these persons have tried sincerely but without success to pursue a line of conduct in keeping with the given directives, they may be safely assured that whoever honestly chooses that course which seems right to him does so in good conscience" (§26).

[27] For background see Janet E. Smith, *Humanae Vitae: A Generation Later* (Washington, DC: Catholic University Press of America, 1991) and William E. May, "The Cultural and Ecclesial Situation 1964–1967: Paving the Way for Dissent from Church Teaching on Contraception," in *Fellowship of Catholic Scholars Quarterly* 32, no. 3 (Fall 2009): 10–19. For another angle, one may read Fr. Charles Curran's own reflections in *Loyal Dissent: Memoir of a Catholic Theologian* (Washington, DC: Georgetown University Press, 2006).

positions, based on a fixed *natura humana*, which are so rigidly defended at this time—be they concerned with marriage, sex, war, and so forth—will remain with us for long. In essence they have been overcome in the doctrinal development at Vatican II.[28]

Similarly, at a conference in Cambridge in 1979 Karl Rahner said that the break between the preconciliar and the postconciliar Church had been as decisive as was the transition from Jewish to Gentile Christianity. By this he meant that the consequence of the break in 1965 would be as far reaching for the Church as was the decision, taken at the Council of Jerusalem in A.D. 49, to allow Gentile Christians.[29] Apparently we had entered a second apostolic age. Christ was refounding his Church. This time around, however, apostolic succession would rest not with bishops but with youthful theologians.

What did the documents really say? Well, for a time this was not seen as the decisive question. Through the 1960s and 1970s the leading interpretation of the council was that the importance of its documents lies not primarily in their letter but in their spirit—in other words, what was thought key to know was not what the texts literally commend but what they one day might countenance. Obviously the Catholic Church is not a democracy, but this does not stop people on occasion from voting with their feet. In response to the revolution that the council precipitated, vote they did—in the millions who never returned. Not since the sixteenth-century Protestant

---

[28] Gregory Baum, *The Credibility of the Church Today: A Reply to Charles Davis* (London: Burns and Oates, 1968), 12, 15.

[29] Tracey Rowland, *Ratzinger's Faith: The Theology of Pope Benedict XVI* (Oxford: Oxford University Press, 2008), 30.

Reformation had the Church seen such an exodus. In the
United States the number of religious sisters fell by one-third
between 1965 and 1985, from 179, 954 to 115, 386 (as of a
recent count there were 59, 601). Today 3,400 parishes in the
United States function without a resident priest, compared
with 549 in 1965.[30] With the decline in priests and religious
most countries have seen a decline in Catholic institutions.
Thus, in English-speaking Canada between 1968 and 1983,
the number of Catholic colleges and universities outside of
Quebec dropped from fifty-seven to seventeen.[31] Religious
observance among Catholics in countries such as the Netherlands virtually disappeared (at present only 7 percent attend
weekly Mass).

[30] These statistics, as well as the figures for Mass attendance in
the Netherlands, are reported on the CARA website (the Center for Applied Research in the Apostolate) at the University
of Georgetown, http://cara.georgetown.edu.

[31] Including Quebec the number of Catholic colleges in 1968
was sixty-three. See E. F. Sheffield, "The Universities of Canada," *Commonwealth Universities Yearbook*, 1969, 1031–1057,
cited in *A Commitment to Higher Education in Canada: The
Report of a Commission of Inquiry on Forty Catholic Colleges and
Universities*, February 1970 (Ottawa: National Education
Office, 1970), 2. For the decline in colleges between 1970
and 1983 see Hogan, "'The Word' and the University World,"
in *Spiritual Roots: Historical Essays on the Roman Catholic Archdiocese of Toronto at 150 Years of Age*, ed. John Duggan, SJ, and
Terry Fay, SJ (Toronto: Our Lady of Lourdes, 1991), 58–72 (particularly 66–70). The *2009 Canadian Catholic Church Directory*
(Montreal: Novalis Publishing, 2009), 54, lists nineteen institutions belonging to the Association of Catholic Colleges and
Universities of Canada (ACCUC). On this, see further R. Topping, "Catholic Studies in Canada: History and Prospects," in
CCHA Historical Studies 76 (2010): 45–60.

The so-called hermeneutic of discontinuity has been much discredited as a result of the last two pontificates, yet there is one date in the history of the council's reception worth noting. In 1985, at the fortieth anniversary of the council's close, John Paul II convened an extraordinary synod of bishops. On the agenda was the review of Vatican II's implementation. In the months leading up to the synod, the Italian journalist Vittorio Messori published a lengthy interview with the prefect of the Congregation for the Doctrine of the Faith titled *The Ratzinger Report*.[32] Open dissent, failing vocations, widespread liturgical abuses had become the norm. What precipitated the crisis? The journalist's report, which became widely known in Rome and elsewhere, made plain the cardinal's mind on some of the causes that led to the present crisis. Perhaps most important, within the interview, Ratzinger openly questioned whether the council, or more specifically its implementation, were not itself partly to blame. The public revelation of the cardinal's mind seemed to set the tone for the synod. Mistakes had been made. The question of the interpretation and implementation of the council had to be recast. Unlike certain traditionalists, and particularly those who followed into schism the French Archbishop Lefebvre (1905–1991), John Paul II remained firmly convinced that the council had been a work of the Holy Spirit. Celebration was called for, certainly; but so was a deepened reflection as to the authentic meaning of the council.

In their addresses to the synod, both John Paul II and Cardinal Ratzinger emphasized paragraph 22 of *Gaudium et Spes* as the

[32] Vittorio Messori, *The Ratzinger Report: An Exclusive Interview on the State of the Church with Joseph Cardinal Ratzinger*, trans. S. Attanasio and G. Harrison (San Francisco: Ignatius Press, 1985).

lens through which to understand the document, and as a key theme of the council. As the early sentences of this section read: in revealing the mystery of the Father and his love, Christ "fully reveals man to himself and brings to light his most high calling." In its dialogue with modernity, therefore, the Church offered to the modern world an answer to its own best questions. Affirming all that is noble in the strivings of modern men and women, and the value of sincere dialogue, she nonetheless never ceases to proclaim Christ. Without Christ the shadows return. Despite humanity's tremendous progress in technology, communications, and even social development, "every man remains a question to himself" (GS 21). By offering Christ to the world, the Church reveals to man what he truly is and establishes criteria according to which any so-called humanism might be judged.

A generation ago many within the Church expected the council to open the way for secular and Christian humanisms to bleed together. Some continue to expect the same. What both the Pope and the head of the Congregation for the Doctrine of the Faith made explicit was that the texts could not be wrested from the Church's abiding Christology. As the Australian theologian Tracy Rowland has observed, by emphasizing *Gaudium et Spes*, paragraph 22, "Both John Paul II and Ratzinger attempted to undercut any secularising potential in the document."[33] If anthropology requires Christology, secular humanism is always inadequate. Hence, as the story of the council's reception unfolds, the bishop's final report marks a point of no return. Tradition, not current intellectual fashion, is to provide the key to conciliar texts:

[33] Tracey Rowland, *Ratzinger's Faith: The Theology of Benedict XVI* (Oxford: Oxford University Press, 2008), 32–33.

It is not licit to separate the pastoral character from the doctrinal vigor of the documents. In the same way, it is not legitimate to separate the spirit and the letter of the Council. Moreover, the Council must be understood in continuity with the great tradition of the Church, and at the same time we must receive light from the Council's own doctrine for today's Church and the men of our time. The Church is one and the same throughout all the councils. (§5)

The year 1985 did not finish the culture wars within the postconciliar Church. But it did signal the beginning of the end of one way of appropriating the reform. If there was any doubt before, it became clear from that time on that the fantasy some had nurtured of a Church remade in their own images was not going to be fulfilled. There could be no radically progressive readings of the council. The 1992 publication of a universal *Catechism of the Catholic Church* only confirmed the same. Catholics have at their disposal all that they need to counter the claims of dissenters. Increasingly, like the disappearance of mainline Protestant Christianity from its once exalted position of influence within North American religion and culture, the old guard of the Catholic *avant garde* would disappear or become disillusioned as they saw that the revolution which they longed to welcome fail to appear.

Two humanisms in conflict

Marking the shifts between *Humanae Vitae* and the extraordinary synod and, after that, even the appearance of the *Catechism*, is one way of describing the reception of the Second Vatican Council; it is one way of describing the rise and fall of a failed attempt to reconcile Christian and secular humanisms. Leaving off the story here, however, might leave a false impression.

Each age nurtures its own vices; one of ours is to substitute images for ideas. It would be easy at this point to read the events of the past forty years—as some do—as a battle between personalities; as a conflict between conservatives and liberals, between good popes and bad bishops, or between daring dissidents and an inflexible institution ("If only the hierarchy could allow women to be priests!"). No doubt, in this history personalities matter. But in the study of doctrine, to reduce principles merely to politics would be simply to miss a great deal. It would be to miss the sun for its reflection or to miss the sea for the waves that happen to lap at your feet. God is, admittedly, bigger than "theology." But that does not mean that theology is untrue. It is only to say that the reality is so much greater than our ability to speak about it, as the real sea is much greater than a map. But we still need the map if we wish to get onto the boat.

Theology is, ultimately, the study not of personalities but of reality—in fact the most real reality of all. Journalism aside, the battles over the reception of the Second Vatican Council cannot be understood in isolation from larger philosophical and cultural trends. Since the late Middle Ages, two visions of humanism have been in competition. In one form God is indispensable; in another he is unnecessary. Anyone who should wish to interpret recent debates over Christology and anthropology would do well to attend to this wider cultural conflict.

One way to gauge what we think about the public character of religion is to observe how we mark time. St. Augustine famously divided the ages of the world into six periods, according to the progress of salvation history.[34] Augustine's division of history held the Western historical imagination for about one thousand years. The dethroning of his division coincided with the beginning of a protracted battle over the right use of symbols in the interpretation of time, the successions we experience in this age, the *saeculum*. Since the Renaissance, the side that sought to invert the Christian symbolism of light and darkness has generally held the upper hand. Consider the term *Dark Ages*. As a description of the period between the years 500 and 1500, you are no longer likely to find the tag applied, except in high school textbooks and on television, yet only yesterday this title served as shorthand for the history of the West from the fall of Rome to the rise of the Protestant Reformers. The name *Dark Ages* was first suggested by Petrarch (1304–1374) and then applied by later humanist scholars as an act of cultural self-definition.[35] By imitating the models of classical Greece and Rome, some humanists saw their age literally as a moment of rebirth, of *renaissance* (hence the French *naissance*, from the Latin *natus*, "birth"). For Petrarch, the Christian centuries marked a time of ignorance, of decay, and of poor

[34] The first age began with Adam and ended with Noah; the second was from Noah to Abraham; the third from Abraham to David; the fourth age ended with the Babylonian captivity; the fifth ended with the birth of Christ; and the sixth and final age, the age of the Church, awaits only the coming of our Lord before the close of all time (*Enchiridion*, 18, 29–34, 45).

[35] On this see Theodore Mommsen, "Petrarch's Conception of the Dark Ages" *Speculum* 17, no. 2 (April 1942): 226–242, where he concludes: Petrarch "plainly distinguishes between three eras: the fortunate ages of the past and, possibly, of the future; between them there is a 'middle' time which has not yet come to an end.... In this sense, then, our modern threefold division of history can be traced back to Petrarch" (p. 241).

Latin style; for the first time since St. Augustine, scholars began to hold up pagan antiquity as an age of "light." The cultural achievements of the pagans, these humanists argued, far surpassed the "darkness" that followed.

Consider another name. The eighteenth century described its epoch as an age of Enlightenment. This time it was not so much the language and art of Christian centuries but their philosophy and politics that were subject to derision. Against faith and authority, the age of revolutions announced the triumph of reason and of liberty. When in 1784 (five years before the French Revolution) Immanuel Kant (1724–1804) penned the manifesto of his age, *Was ist Aufklärung? (What is Enlightenment?)*, he promised that "for this Enlightenment, however,

Allegorical Portrait of Petrarch, Italian, sixteenth century, engraving

nothing is required but freedom." Despite their differences, Friedrich Hegel (1770–1883), John Stuart Mill (1806–1875), and Karl Marx (1818–1883) all agreed that historical progress should be defined according to the wider reign of *freedom*. Progress required emancipation from authority, most of all, from the authority of religion. What the leading eighteenth- and nineteenth-century social philosophers attempted to construct was a society founded, in short, without reference to the authority of the God of Jesus Christ. This was the dream and great gamble of the modern project.

In many respects, the terms of postconciliar debate were defined already two hundred years ago by eighteenth-century social philosophers. To give one instance, in his work *Perpetual Peace*, Kant proposed that a state could be ordered "even by a nation of devils," by which he meant that peace could be achieved apart from virtue with appeal only to enlightened self-interest.[36] On this view, statecraft requires only that the mechanisms of human nature be properly understood and then manipulated. God disappears. Man is finally come of age and left alone, but he is lonesome. As Kant argued: if only the natural laws that govern pleasure and pain can be directed, self-interested and otherwise antagonistic individuals could be compelled to submit to the coercive force of law. Even without goodwill Kant promised peace among men. We, of course, pay a price for this mastery. The cost of a purely secular politics is what the twentieth-century Jewish political philosopher Leo Strauss (1899–1973) called our "oblivion of eternity." Estrangement from our deepest desire was the high cost that we had to

---

[36] Immanuel Kant, *Perpetual Peace*, first supplement, in *Perpetual Peace and Other Essays*, trans. T. Humphrey (Indianapolis, Indiana: Hackett Publishing, 1983).

suffer for attempting to be absolutely sovereign over nature.[37] The United Nations, secular with respect to its foundation, eschatological with respect to its ambition, is quite literally Immanuel Kant's fantasy come alive.

Of course there are others who do not share this dream. Since the beginning of the modern era there have been fundamentally two secular humanisms with which the Church is in conflict. The Church can side neither with those secular philosophers who accept nor with those who reject Kant's proposal. In politics, as in many other realms, the Church offers herself as a third way between stubborn alternatives. What distinguishes the culture wars of late modernity, however, is that the terms of the conflict have altered. Now, even those who agree with Kant (those who agree, in other words, that politics should be founded without God) no longer accept the Christian ethic that he presumed. Friedrich Nietzsche (1844–1900), the founder of postmodernism, very perceptively called Kant the great delayer.[38] In his view, the consequence of Kant's genius was to fool Europeans into accepting the terms of Enlightenment modernity without acknowledging the bloodless sacrifice that they had performed. Killing men is only a little more gruesome than killing their God. Relegating religion to the sphere of private morality mitigated the conflict between Christian and secular humanisms, although only for a time. Once the mighty tide of religion retreated, the economy, the law, the hospital,

---

[37] See Leo Straus, *What Is Political Philosophy? And Other Essays* (Chicago: University of Chicago Press, 1988), 55.

[38] See *Ecce Homo* on "The Case of Wagner," §2, where Kant and Leibniz are singled out for their moralism as "*diese zwei grössten Hemmschuhe der intellektuellen Rechtschaffenheit Europa's!*" ("these two greatest brake pads of intellectual honesty in Europe").

the regiment—in short, all those institutions through which we regulate temporal affairs—were left exposed before the hot sun of self-interest. This retreat granted to the secular a naked isolation. The terms of this fragile peace could last so long as the precepts of Christian morality remained. These precepts no longer remain—at least not as a shared body of assumptions. The steady roll of anti-Christian and anti-life legislation in the name of human rights that pours forth from our courts from Strasbourg to Canada's Human Rights Commissions to the United State's Equal Employment Opportunity Commission has become evidence enough to convince even the most unbelieving.[39]

[39] Some of the more bizarre rulings of these North American Commissions have now become more widely known. In Canada, one thinks of the British Columbia Human Rights Tribunal decision *Nixon v. Vancouver Rape Relief*. In 1995 Kimberly Nixon, a male-to-female transvestite, applied to volunteer as a counselor at the Vancouver Rape Relief Center (VRR). Understandably, Nixon's application was denied. The VRR accepts women volunteers only. Nixon had undergone a sex-change surgery and had his ID switched to "male" by the provincial British Columbia government. Still, the VRR declined the offer. They recognized that many traumatized women would feel uncomfortable sharing their concerns with a six-foot-tall athletic-looking (former) male. Nixon disagreed. He took the matter before the Human Rights Commission, and won. After more than five years, a twenty-one-day hearing, and a legal bill of over $150,000, VRR was ordered to pay $7,500 in "damages" to Nixon. As Heather McNaughton wrote in the Tribunal's judgment, the VRR had denied Nixon the "opportunity to participate fully and freely in the economic, social, political, and cultural life of BC." (The tribunal's ruling has since been overturned by a higher court.) This and other such cases are documented in Ezra Levant's *Shakedown: How Our Government Is Undermining Democracy in the Name of Human Rights* (Toronto: McClelland and Stewart, 2009). In the United States, one

Indeed, from the vantage of the twenty-first century, the most articulate proponents of both sides of the divide now equally wonder how we could have accepted the compromise for so long. Both secular and Christian humanists have come to recognize that, without God, even the horizon of our moral judgments is wiped out. The terms of good and evil are no longer fixed. Man sails upon a sea without a sky above. But, oddly, even this emancipation has not freed us from the tyranny of morality. The modern world is full of crusades: liberating ourselves from public religion has not freed us from the old impulse to prejudice. Privatizing religion has not freed us from bigotry; it has not rescued us from being "judgmental." We have abandoned morality. We have not ceased to be moralists.

The steady stream of campaigners for everything from tree rights to turkey rights never permits us to forget this oppressive tax required of citizens of a global, enlightened age.

> *Turning and turning in the widening gyre*
> *The falcon cannot hear the falconer;*
> *Things fall apart; the centre cannot hold;*
> *Mere anarchy is loosed upon the world,*
> *The blood-dimmed tide is loosed, and everywhere*
> *The ceremony of innocence is drowned;*
> *The best lack all conviction, while the worst*
> *Are full of passionate intensity.*

This is Yeats (1865–1939) in *The Second Coming* on the anarchy of the First World War. Even as the Second World War

---

might cite the Federal Equal Opportunity Commission's 2009 ruling against the Catholic Belmont Abbey College for failing to provide coverage for contraception in its health insurance policy for employees.

ground to a halt, there were many who worried about the order that would follow the peace. In Catholic political theory leading figures in the mid-twentieth century sought to find common ground between Christians and nonbelievers. They thought they had found what they were searching for in the language of human rights. The French philosopher Jacques Maritain and American Jesuit John Courtney Murray both pinned the future on rights-talk. What they hoped was that such language could provide a center of gravity for all men of goodwill to gather around; "human rights," they proposed, could supply a way of speaking substantial enough to support the notion of human dignity, but not bearing the metaphysical weight that unbelievers might refuse to carry.

Today the wisdom of such a compromise is less clear. In contemporary political discourse the doctrine of human rights survives as the last vestige of the Christian natural-law tradition. Here is a case where the new wine threatens to burst the old wineskins. Separated from its older sources in Scripture and Christian philosophy, contemporary human rights doctrine has lost some of its body. In his 2008 address to the United Nations on the sixtieth anniversary of the *Universal Declaration of Human Rights*, Pope Benedict warned of the danger of severing the language of rights from the affirmation of the human person as the privileged high point of God's creation. Such rights are

> based on the natural law inscribed on human hearts and present in different cultures and civilizations. Removing human rights from this context would mean restricting their range and yielding to a relativistic conception, according to which the meaning and interpretation of rights could vary and their universality would be denied

in the name of different cultural, political, social and even religious outlooks. This great variety of viewpoints must not be allowed to obscure the fact that not only rights are universal, but so too is the human person, the subject of those rights.[40]

We will take up natural law in our discussion of Part 3 of the *Catechism*, but here we note that the purpose of the theory is to express our natural apprehension of good and evil. Natural law is natural in the sense that all people can have access to it; it is law inasmuch as its precepts present themselves as binding moral norms, first among which is the obligation to do good and avoid evil. Simply by virtue of our nature as rational creatures, there are certain norms that we know we should not transgress. There is one other feature to note. The very possibility of there being something natural presumes such a thing as a fixed nature. This conviction is no longer widely shared. Benedict XVI's claim before the UN—a theme he would memorably return to in 2011 before the German Bundestag—was that once we exclude God, our perceptions of human nature, of justice, and of human dignity begin to unravel. Blot out the sun, and the moon loses its luster; cancel the Creator, and it only follows that creatures lose the *imago*. In a godless universe, human will finds itself left with no direction, no first impulse, and no tether to serve as a guide. Matter, including our own, becomes little more than dull clay that the strong are free to manipulate. In short, when God is gone, nature is going. Without absolute justice, "rights" easily serve wrongs. Far from protecting individuals, in

---

[40] "Service to the human family: address to the UN General Assembly," in *Christ Our Hope: Homilies and Addresses in USA* (London: Catholic Truth Society, 2008), 50.

such a climate the appeal to such language easily turns against the dignity of the person.

Certainly, the deployment of the language of human rights is far more hazardous today than sixty years ago. Regardless of the difficulties inherent in persuading other nations to embrace the idea of inviolable human rights, even in the West the theological basis for such a doctrine has all but eroded. After the fall of Berlin's walls in 1989 there were left standing no serious military threats to liberal democracy. Even today neither China nor the Middle East poses a credible challenge to NATO. What threatens the West more than falling bombs or collapsing markets is the failure of our own courage. We are like the man who set off a detonation and is suddenly terrified by the tumbling snow. We are losing a war of ideas first of all because we tried to get God out of our heads, removing him from the classroom and from the houses of government. Without a Creator, there can be no doctrine of creation; without creation nature itself loses its status as a norm for action, and even a guide to reality. Without God we are even losing the will to believe that most elementary of creeds: the wild and mystical faith that the world is real and that truth exists.

Does the notion of objective truth undermine freedom? This is what secularists fear about faith. No, to be free does not mean to flounder. Genuine freedom could never mean simply "doing what you want." To do good, you must know something about what is good, which is precisely what the skeptic says we cannot know. That would be only to consign us to the tiniest of all prisons—ourselves. When the most elementary faith fails, faith in the mind, you do not thereby make yourself freer. The public school student who is abandoned to believe that $4 \times 4 = 8$ is not liberated from the multiplication table but merely made a slave to the calculations of every dishonest employer. The teenage girl who is free to believe that her chastity is not sacred does not liberate herself from parents, but enslaves herself to the lusts of adolescent boys. It is likewise with the citizen: to believe that values are merely the product of culture does not make you free from prejudice, but only removes you as one less obstacle to the tyrant. Apart from the objectivity of moral law, citizens literally have no reason to oppose the tyrant's will. For then, justice would be only the will of the stronger.

In all these cases the flight from authority, even the authority of the mind, leads not to enlightenment but to a brutal conformity. This situation is what Pope Benedict has called the "dictatorship of relativism."[41] Seen in this light, what threatens the private lives and public institutions of the West are not external dangers but internal collapse. We no longer find it surprising that there should be almost total uniformity among our elites on questions of social ethics (say, regarding stem-cell research or euthanasia). What is striking is that they agitate for legal changes usually on the basis of universal human rights.

As Nietzsche well recognized, the roots of the new humanism spring not even from the eighteenth-century liberal tradition but from the sandy soils of relativism. Young activists usually do not know this. This is true in part because of a lack

---

[41] From his homily at the Vatican Basilica, April 18, 2005: "Today, having a clear faith based on the Creed of the Church is often labeled as fundamentalism. Whereas relativism, that is, letting oneself be 'tossed here and there, carried about by every wind of doctrine,' seems the only attitude that can cope with modern times. We are building a dictatorship of relativism that does not recognize anything as definitive and whose ultimate goal consists solely of one's own ego and desires."

of education. But there is also a psychological explanation. Nietzsche called the West's new humanists "the last men."[42] This is his euphemism for secular liberal democrats. The last men are people who have retained the language of science and morality but fail to recognize the consequences of jettisoning God. Without God the language of objective science and universal values turns into a fiction. With no first cause and no final end, science and morality are merely willed projections. The last men have killed God but do not have legs sturdy enough to stand while the tremors follow. Philosophers calmly explain to their classes that truth is a fiction and then wonder why students cheat. Sociologists tell men that they should act like women and wonder why children have no fathers. Parents leave their children to make up their own minds and wonder why their offspring conduct themselves like slaves: obsessed with fashion, manipulated by advertising, bored. Such enlightened progressives literally are "the last men" because they enjoy a liberty founded upon a social order that they have labored to dismantle. And so, the new philosophy of license and unlimited tolerance is defended, ironically, in the old language of justice and right.

People of my grandparents' generation remember how the new ethic first made its appearances in law. They recall how the legislation that opened the door to Canada's cultural revolution was Pierre Elliot Trudeau's omnibus bill of 1968–1969. At a stroke, contraception, abortion, and gambling became tolerable to all as the fruit of Trudeau's vision of the so-called *Just Society*. When in 2005 Canada became the third nation in the world to extend the privilege of marriage to gay couples, it was again a

[42] See *Thus Spoke Zarathustra*, 1.5.

On the Creed

Roman Catholic politician (Paul Martin) who made it happen. The prime minister knew, as everyone knew, that if taken to a national referendum, the law would not pass. And no vote was taken. Here was the twist. As a politician, Martin was responsible enough to state his reason for denying a vote: recognition of gay marriage was a matter of *natural* justice. The success of the bill meant a defense of universal human rights. But, surely, even those who applaud the prime minister's courage might wonder at his language. Americans, Britons, Australians, and others are now bombarded with the same claim. Christians and men of goodwill everywhere need to offer a thoughtful response: Does it really make sense to argue for gay marriage on the basis of rights? How do such politicians know that such unions are natural?

Gay marriage is certainly not "natural" under biological descriptions (since it is by design infertile) any more than it is "natural" in the sense of belonging to custom (since no religious tradition has ever countenanced it). From the parliamentary transcript, one discovers that the prime minister appealed to nature in no ordinary sense. What he evoked was, rather, a complex recently constructed theory about nature. Natural justice in the minds of such men has become the sum of abstract *equality* plus unlimited *liberty* backed by state-enforced *tolerance* — or, in essence, when John Locke and Nietzsche run the house with Mike the Mountie on guard at the front door. The sum of justice defined in this way turns out to be scribbled upon a check that no real bank would accept, since it is of the sort that can be continually re-presented with new figures.

Of course, not only politicians are to blame. Many good-hearted folks fail to see that when the substance of natural law disappears, when good and evil vanish as fixed reference points, it is no longer justice that is being debated in Houses of Parliament and Senates but the law of the jungle.

Over one hundred years ago Nietzsche made sport of the contradictions inherent in the ideas of contemporary humanists. What he helps us to see is that the radical left's appeal to the language of rights today only obfuscates their true philosophical position to be made manifest tomorrow. Such language will be dropped when it no longer serves their purposes. What is at stake in the West's cultural crisis is not, for instance, the correct balance between a mother's right to privacy and her child's right to life. What is at stake, rather, is whether man must take into account the God of Jesus Christ in the ordering of society. This is the only fundamental question for the social philosophy of the future. Our answer will determine whether our civilization will sink into Hell or merely suffer through a long Purgatory.

Here ends our historical survey. The *Catechism*'s key claim in relation to the contemporary conflict between humanisms is this: without Christ, true progress halts; ignore Christ, and our humanity is forgotten. If Catholic culture is the outgrowth of Christian humanism, and if that humanism is founded upon the doctrine of Christ, remove the God-man, and the edifice crashes. Make the Gospel merely amenable to unbelievers, and all the towering cathedrals, soaring polyphony, and sturdy statues of David come tumbling down into one vast glittering mound of rubble. Although throughout the twentieth century the Catholic Church has been a vigorous defender of the language of human rights, sixty years after the United Nations' *Universal Declaration of Human Rights*, it has become more evident that humanism without Christ descends into an inhuman humanism (cf. CV 78).

On the Creed

The God of faith and reason

The Christian argument for faith is no argument against philosophy, but it is an argument for the reasonableness of religion. Having identified the two humanisms in conflict, I would like now to suggest why orthodox religion remains our best hope for guarding joy in an age sunk in sadness. In Christology, as in every branch of sacred science, the higher springs from the lower. Christ's divinity had to be revealed to us and must be believed by faith, yet the Church always addresses herself to man foremost as a bearer of *reason*. With regard to God's existence, from St. Paul forward, Catholics have been struck by man's irresistibly intuitive, even primal, awareness of the Creator (cf. Rom. 1:19). Ethnographers tell us that every indigenous nation has embedded within its mythology the belief in a supreme Creator, as our own Native Americans have; studies done by child psychologists too suggest that theism is the pre-reflective, or default, position of young children.[43] Psalm 119

---

[43] On this see particularly the work of Justin Barrett, Senior Researcher at Oxford's Centre for Anthropology and Mind. The standard model held by developmental psychologists until recently has followed Jean Piaget (1896–1980), who held that children form beliefs about God by projecting and magnifying attributes of adults onto a superhuman person. In terms of the formation of children's concepts, recent and more detailed studies have begun to contradict this hypothesis. Evidence suggests, rather, that children have a predisposition to see the natural world as designed by a creator. Contra Richard Dawkins, studies in developmental psychology suggest not that children have to be indoctrinated into belief, but that they are born with it, that they are "cognitively equipped from early on to develop concepts of God (and other humans) independently of their concepts of people" (R. A. Richert and J. L. Barrett, "Do You See What I See? Young Children's Assumptions about

tells that the heavens declare the glory of God, and these sweet lines by the New England poet Emily Dickinson (1830–1886) capture something of this innocence:

> I never saw a moor,
> I never saw the sea,
> Yet know I how the heather looks,
> And what a wave must be.
>
> I never spoke with God,
> Nor visited in heaven;
> Yet certain am I of the spot
> As if a chart were given.

Although many professional academics regard natural theology as naive, in virtually all periods except our own, the reverse was true. Ancient Greek, and Roman, medieval Arabic and European, and even early modern philosophers nearly all regarded God's existence as rationally demonstrable. Since Vatican I (1870) this conviction has been also a point of Catholic dogma. Reflecting this, the *Catechism* proposes for belief certain articles that, by its own admission, can be the object either of faith or of reason.

In the Catholic system there is distinction but not separation between faith and reason. What does this tell us about the nature of our Creed? According to the old formula, grace presupposes nature (*gratia praesupponit naturum*) (cf. *Summa Theologica*, I, Q. 2, art. 2); grace perfects, it does not destroy. The Church

---

God's Perceptual Abilities," in *International Journal for the Psychology of Religion* 15, no. 4 (2005): 284). For further evidence of the naturalness of theism see J. Barrett's *Why Would Anyone Believe in God?* (Walnut Creek, California: Alta Mira, 2004).

New England Farm in Winter, American, nineteenth century, oil on canvas

affirms that reason alone can tell us that God exists, if we will listen. The trouble is we often do not listen. Even the little that we may know needs to be purified. We need natural knowledge of God, but it is neither complete nor sufficient on its own. As St. Thomas Aquinas says at the opening of his *Summa Theologica* (I, Q. 1, art. 1), apart from revelation knowledge of God would have been grasped "by only a few, after a long time, and with the admixture of many errors" (*a paucis, per longum tempus, et cum admixtione multorum errorum*). For Aquinas there are, indeed, three ascending degrees of knowledge of God. The first is the natural knowledge we can achieve by reflection upon the world; the second is what we know through revelation; the third is the vision of heaven, "when the mind will be elevated to gaze perfectly upon the things revealed" (*Summa Contra Gentiles*, 4.1).

When the *Catechism* speaks of our natural knowledge of God (or of the moral law, for that matter) it does not extend to reason and nature a sphere of absolute independence. The Church, unlike postmodern philosophers, affirms the integrity of our natural knowledge. Unlike characteristically modern philosophers, the Church denies that this is sufficient. Although Thomists and masters of the *nouvelle théologie* (the two contemporary schools of Catholic thought that support the conclusions of the Magisterium on disputed moral questions) are divided over other matters, they are united on this one: if in one moment the Church concedes the natural knowledge of God (CCC 31), at the next she registers nature's inadequacies (CCC 37). If at one moment she celebrates man's religiosity (CCC 28), at the next she warns that he is always forgetting about God because of sin (CCC 29), or even just because the Olympics happen to be on television. It takes so little to distract us.

Desire and knowledge of God are natural in the same way that desire and knowledge of calculus are natural: anyone can learn it. Left to our own devices, however, few will learn; without a gifted teacher, even fewer will take an interest in logarithms, let alone try to understand how they were derived. How far, precisely, this distinction between nature and grace should be pressed would become highly contested in the last decades before the Second Vatican Council. To a limited extent the range of possible answers to that question is even reflected in the council documents. The question whether nature, and correspondingly matters pertaining to our life in this age, can be ordered without explicit reference to Christ, bore heavily upon the interpretations of the council texts in the years during its immediate reception, and in the years that followed.

Christology and culture

As we mentioned, alongside the Enlightenment tradition now reigns its negative image, the rule of anti-reason, of the postmodern. Thus it is common to hear the Church criticized from opposite points of view: professional eastern gurus and otherwise spiritual people are forever calling Catholicism too rational; at the same time, more run-of-the-mill agnostics complain that the Church is not reasonable enough. And there is just enough truth in the critics' claims to make the bystander wonder. At one moment the Church does appear the champion of universal reason (so suggesting the possibility of humanism without Christ); but then at the next she declares her poverty apart from grace (so rendering such a suggestion void). In any given week, the Pope is likely to address the United Nations on Monday and then pray with pilgrims at Lourdes on Friday. You can almost watch the disjunction form under some people's furrowed brows: Is the Church for or against reason? Obviously, this way of putting the matter is a false start. From the Catholic point of view, it is not either faith or reason, but both. There is distinction without division. Just because Richard Dawkins is a declared enemy does not make Deepak Chopra your friend.

Returning to our opening question: Why does Christology matter? Without Christ no true Enlightenment is possible—either for individuals or for societies. Shadows do indeed return: man loses both God and himself. At the Second Vatican Council, at the 1985 extraordinary synod, as throughout her history, the Church has guarded her creed because it is the pearl of great price. Like a massive cathedral, Catholic belief and practice rests on her confession of Jesus Christ, "the cornerstone" (Eph. 2:20). Indeed, the first seven ecumenical councils, from Nicaea I in 325 to Nicaea II in 787, were each called primarily to settle christological debates. With ever sharpening precision the Church like a good teacher explained, defended, and explored the claim that Christ "became truly man while remaining truly God" (CCC 464). Both sides of the equation need to hold. Lose either, and the world falls apart, man becomes either a ghost or an ape. As the *Catechism* notes:

> Because "human nature was assumed, not absorbed," in the mysterious union of the incarnation, the Church was led over the course of centuries to confess the full reality of Christ's human soul, with its operations of intellect and will, and of his human body. In parallel fashion, she had to recall on each occasion that Christ's human nature belongs, as his own, to the divine person of the Son of God, who assumed it. (CCC 470; quoting GS 22)

That little phrase "assumed, not absorbed" is taken from the same paragraph of *Gaudium et Spes* of which we spoke earlier, number 22. But as we might expect, its origin is much older. In the thirteenth century St. Thomas Aquinas wrote that Christ "assumed our nature" so that he might make us gods (*Opusculum*, 57:1–4; CCC 460). Before that we might look to St. Athanasius in the fourth century, St. Irenaeus in the second, and to 2 Peter 1:4 (cf. CCC 460). By stating that Christ "assumed our nature" St. Thomas summed up the trajectory of a long biblical and patristic tradition that affirmed Christ's divinity as much as his humanity.

In terms of official teaching, Catholic Christology is better settled today than it ever has been in her long history. Why, then, at least at the level of the parish, does confusion about doctrine so often persist? A striking weakness of contemporary Catholicism has been, quite plainly, its failure to catechize. What has frayed the cloth of Catholic culture is not so much corruption of dogma as a failure of its transmission. This is why Cardinal Francis George, among others, has emphasized that it is not sufficient only to explain what is good about Catholicism; you also need to point out the errors that would distort the picture. Apologetics, in other words, needs once again to take its place amid catechesis.[44] Our deference to the principle of dialogue has largely overwhelmed our passion for debate, and unsurprisingly, heresy abounds.

If we need to revive a culture of spirited debate what, in matters christological, should we wish to debate about? As a test question we might ask: What part of Catholic Christology is most scandalous? Presumably, the claim that Jesus is God. Modern sensibility has not turned its back (yet) on Jesus the emotional healer; nor does it have a problem with Jesus the pacifist or the liberator of women. Worthy as these images of Christ are, in isolation they are inadequate. Heard from unoffending pulpits these fragments tend to reinforce familiarity with the user-friendly Jesus and not much else. The salvific character of Christ's work is lost; so too is his divine nature. Some measure of the times can be gauged by the outcry raised over the declaration *Dominus Iesus* issued in 2000 by the Congregation for the Doctrine of the Faith, a document which merely reaffirmed the traditional understanding of Christ's unique position as Savior.[45] Interestingly, where modern heretics find it incredible

---

[44] See Cardinal Francis George, *The Difference God Makes: A Catholic Vision of Faith, Communion and Culture* (New York: Crossroads, 2010).

[45] Against those who shy away from speaking of the uniqueness of Christ, the document noted that Catholics "can and must say that Jesus Christ has a significance and a value for the human race and its history, which are unique and singular, proper to him alone, exclusive, universal, and absolute" (DI 15). On the related question of the Church's universality as the ark of salvation for the world, we read that the unity of the

that Christ could have been a god, ancients found it difficult to believe that Christ was truly a man. The first-century Gnostics as much as the eighth-century iconoclasts were united in the suspicion that, somehow, the God of light could not mix with a body of flesh, at least not without either polluting the one or overwhelming the other.

In ancient as well as in modern times, christological heresies have proceeded along two well-worn paths. One has led people to compromise Christ's humanity, the other his divinity. These represent, as it were, the Platonic and Aristotelian forms that heresy has taken down the ages. The Platonic, which tends to regard Christ exclusively as divine, is represented by the heretical fourth-century Bishop of Laodicea, Apollinarius (c. 310– c. 390). Of Christ Apollinarius asserted "the divine Word had replaced the soul" (CCC 471). Against this, the Church reasoned that since Christ was true man, he too must have had a rational soul, like us. The problem with Apollinarius's view, and other such over-Platonising tendencies, is that Christ ends up only *appearing* human, seeming to have become man. Christ's flesh becomes an outer garment that merely clothed the god within. To hold such is not Catholic. Nor is it properly humane. As Gregory Nazianzus vigorously argued, if Christ only looked like a man, then there would be some part of our humanity that remains unassumed and therefore unredeemed.[46]

Church is not simply an eschatological reality, but a present fact: "The Catholic faithful *are required to profess* that there is an historical continuity—rooted in apostolic succession —between the Church founded by Christ and the Catholic Church" (emphasis in original) (DI 16).

[46] Cf. S. W. Need, *Truly Human and Truly Divine: The Story of Christology and the Seven Ecumenical Councils* (Peabody, Massachusetts: Hendrickson Publishers, 2008), 71–72. In modern

On the Creed

Christological heresies can also arise from the opposite direction. To the other side of the philosophical divide, Aristotelian heresies have imagined Christ as an inspiring human being but one not in truth divine. In antiquity, Arius (250–336) was the model spokesman of this view. Although Arius and his followers divided the Church and the empire in the fourth century, his heresy would not resurface again as a serious threat for nearly a millennium and a half, in the eighteenth century. Suddenly the Aristotelian form of the heresy reappeared with all the ravenousness of a bear awakened in spring. In philosophical anthropology, this opposite tendency to reduce man to his body is represented in Hume, in Marx, and probably by your high school biology teacher.

Today both habits of thought mingle and compete. If the nineteenth-century idealist philosophers and Romantic poets exulted in the immaterial in man, and the twentieth-century materialists triumphed in his brute animality, within contemporary culture these anthropologies are given vigorous and contradictory expression. Thus, on the one hand, too many among the middle classes sacrifice all to the altar of low-grade-desire satisfaction. Wal-Mart dominates. In this way our humanity has been reduced to the level of the consumer who seeks salvation from the gods of fashion, of commerce, of travel, in the temples of the mall, the bank, and the Mexican resort. Health has become our obsession (since pleasure is impossible apart from it); we fear the germs we cannot see in the way that older men feared the demons that they could not touch.

---

philosophy the tendency to disregard the goodness of embodied existence in favor of mind was carried forward by the idealist tradition in Descartes, Hegel, and Berkeley.

Everybody can see that the materialist sets the tonic note, but to this dominant key there is a minor seventh. Alongside this reductionism thrives a party of discord, attractive particularly among many affluent youth. Here is the anthropology of a world-denying asceticism. This is the antihumanism of the overpopulation gurus, and the transhumanism of the bioengineers. Modern idealists will despise man—consuming, smelly, wrinkly man —who stomps along the earth leaving behind his fat carbon footprints. This sort of idealist despises that part of man which cannot transcend his mere earthly existence. There are points of agreement between these two groups. When freedom is ever at stake, the new pagans, like the old, have little trouble with leaving their unwanted young and their unwanted old to die. C. S. Lewis once suggested that the apotheosis of the modern pagan would be neither a strict materialist nor a new-age spiritualist but a fusion of the two: the materialist idealist, Lewis's Dr. Weston in *The Voyage to Venus*, the second book of his space trilogy.

If there is one lesson to draw from our survey of contemporary Christology it is this: Christology matters because without it, without that marvelous balance of contraries which is Catholic orthodoxy, man loses God, man loses himself, man even loses the right to walk upon the ground beneath his feet. The resources of our age have not allowed modern man, it would seem, to be capable of using nature without abusing her or of respecting Mother Earth without bowing down to worship at her dusty feet. For all its passionate intensity, nothing in the new environmentalism has been able to recreate the sacramental vision of the enchanted world that Catholics know and cannot forget to love. It is to that vision that we turn our attention to next.

St. Michael the Archangel, David Clayton

On Worship:
How Liturgy Transforms

The Mass of the Ages

The best way to understand what an institution believes is to observe what its members do. Parents of young children instinctively know this. A mother who wishes to learn what her local elementary school thinks about discipline asks first to see not a handbook, but a classroom. What does Miss Smith expect from her students during a reading lesson? The surest way to find out is to watch her conduct one. The same is true for doctrine. Few people have a healthy appetite for academic theology, but most Catholics periodically do find themselves in a pew. What do they observe? It is here, in the church, in its architecture, its sacred images, its candles, its incense, its music, its priests, its people—in short, it is through all the stone, color, smell, sound, and movement which gives form to the liturgy—that believers and unbelievers alike discover what Catholics think about the glory of the Lord.

Unlike Protestant worship, Catholic liturgy never simply looks to the past. There is no lost golden age for the Church. Through the sacraments Christ is present to the Church no less today than when he walked through Jerusalem. The Sacrifice

65

of the Mass, whereby Christ's continual presence through the liturgy is made present, is that action most highly regarded by Roman Catholics and at the same time the most severely scorned by unbelievers. To the incredulous, the worship of a tiny wafer is just one more testament to how deep into darkness the religious imagination can sink. But to Catholics, it is otherwise. Admit that there is a God, and it follows that he could visit the world; admit that he came once robed in flesh, and why not a thousand times more in bread? As John Dryden (1631–1700) has it in *The Hind and the Panther*, published one year after his conversion to Roman Catholicism in 1686:

> Could he his god-head veil with flesh and blood
> And not veil these again to be our food?
> His grace both is equal in extent,
> The first affords us life, the second nourishment.
>
> (Bk. 1, lines 134–137)

In the Roman empire Christians regularly had to defend themselves against the charge of cannibalism, as Athenagoras did before Marcus Aurelius in A.D. 176 (*Apology*, 31–36). Perhaps the earliest account of Christian worship is offered by St. Justin Martyr, in a letter to the pagan emperor Antonius Pius around the year 155. In Justin's *First Apology* the basic structure of the Mass is already manifest. We have the reading of the Apostles' writings, the homily, intercessory prayer, a kiss of peace, and then "someone brings bread and a cup of water and wine mixed together to him who presides over the brethren." The rite concludes with thanksgiving, with prayers, and with the bread and wine consumed (CCC 1345; quoting from St. Justin Martyr's *First Apology*, 65–67). This haunting sacrifice has been a continual source of strength for Christians down the centuries. As Blessed John Henry Newman wrote of Catholic worship in his 1848 work *Loss and Gain*:

> To me nothing is so consoling, so piercing, so thrilling, so overcoming, as the Mass, said as it is among us. I could attend Masses for ever and not be tired. It is not a mere form of words — it is a great action, the greatest action that can be on earth. It is, not the invocation merely, but, if I dare use the word, the evocation of the Eternal. He becomes present on the altar in flesh and blood, before whom angels bow and devils tremble. This is that awful event which is the scope, and is the interpretation, of every part of the solemnity.[47]

It is a fact not unrelated to the collapse of Catholic culture that few among us experience worship that answers to this description. For laypeople, perhaps the most disappointing effect of the liturgical reform has been a lessening of expectations as to what liturgy will accomplish for our spiritual growth. Simply put, fewer and fewer Catholics think it worth their while to show up on Sunday morning. In English-speaking Canada, for instance, in 1957 weekly attendance for Catholics was 75 percent (88 in Quebec); by 1975 that figure had fallen to 48 percent; these days about 29 percent of Catholics fulfill their Sunday obligation.[48] Weekly church attendance among

---

[47] John Henry Newman, *Loss and Gain: The Story of a Convert* (London: Longmans, Green and Co., 1906), pt. 2, ch. 20, 327–328.

[48] For these figures see Reginald Bibby, *Restless Gods: The Renaissance of Religion in Canada* (Toronto: Novalis, 2004), 20, and "The Catholic Situation in North America: Magnificent Opportunities, Breathtaking Responsibility," in *Journal of Mission Studies* XIV (2007): 69–84.

Notre Dame Basilica, Montreal

Catholics in the United States follows a similar pattern, but remains higher at 38 percent; in the United Kingdom it sits at 17 percent, in France at 12 percent.[49] Why this waning interest in Catholic ritual?

Among the several causes, I wish to address two. The first is a deficit in our understanding (which I explore below), the second (which I explore in the next chapter) a deficit in our presentation of Catholic liturgy. Liturgy and the sacraments are the continuation of Christ's incarnation among us. Indeed, according to the *Catechism*, the Church most supremely acts for the salvation of the world in her worship. Where the first part of the *Catechism* focuses on the foundations of Christian life in the Creed, the second explores its implications for our worship. According to an ancient expression, the *lex orandi* (the rule

[49] These figures are given on the CARA website: http://cara. georgetown.edu.

of prayer) and the *lex credendi* (the rule of belief) are mutually informing. Said otherwise, "The Church believes as she prays" (CCC 1124). Inasmuch as our actions flow from our beliefs, if the above holds true, then our rule of prayer has the power to shape culture as well, "the whole way of life of a people." In what follows I hope to illuminate how this is true—how liturgy shapes our common life. Since liturgy, our immersion in the web of sacramental signs, transforms faith, every action that disturbs cult produces an equal and often disastrous effect on culture. Revive cult, and culture will eventually follow.

Liturgy since Vatican II

Both the theory and practice of Catholic worship has been the object of experimentation in the decades since the council. Any evaluation of the gains and losses that have attended Catholic worship since the reforms of Vatican II would have to take into account the larger Liturgical Movement of which the council was in many respects the fruition. As a way into our discussion it will be useful to offer a brief history of the movement.

We can divide the modern Liturgical Movement into three phases. The first phase began in the eighteenth century; the second went from the late nineteenth up to Pius XII's encyclical on liturgical reform, *Mediator Dei*, in 1947; the third was from 1948 to the Second Vatican Council. Prominent in the nineteenth century were figures such as Dom Prosper Guéranger (1805–1875), the re-founder and abbot of the famous French Abbey of Solesmes, and, in the twentieth century, the Munich-based theologian Romano Guardini (1885–1968). The English liturgical scholar Alcuin Reid concludes in *The Organic Development of the Liturgy* (2005) that in general the Movement aimed at restoring liturgical piety of the faithful. What did this mean? In practical terms, priests promoted active participation in the liturgy by distributing liturgical books among the laity. Throughout the nineteenth century publishing houses produced all manner of devotional materials: during the 1860s congregational singing of Gregorian chant was encouraged in Italy; a Latin-French missal was published in 1882; and studies such as Guéranger's fifteen-volume (unfinished) "L'Annee liturgique" and his 1885 collected conferences *On the Holy Mass* sought to bring the faithful closer to the prayers of the Church.[50] The Church's pastors hoped that a more intelligent participation in the liturgy would help counteract the secularizing influence of the modern age.

Ironically the call for the "active participation of the faithful" has been deployed for opposite purposes. *Sacrosanctum Concilium*, the Second Vatican Council's Constitution on the Liturgy, and following this, the *Catechism*, certainly affirm that "Catholics should have full, conscious, active participation in the liturgy" (CCC 1030; citing SC 23). However, *participatio actuosa* quickly became identified with external movement rather than an interior action, prayer. Where the older Liturgical Movement had sought to increase the participation of the faithful by a deepened understanding of the prayer of the Mass, the more recent trend simply encouraged people to become busy, and along the way to blur the distinction between priest and people. If laypeople are going to participate in the Mass, so the thinking goes, then not everything should be left to one man. To be involved is to *do* things such as reading, welcoming, directing, and even distributing Communion. In the name of the council, many have taken this tiny phrase to endorse

[50] Discussed in Alcuin Reid, *The Organic Development of the Liturgy* (San Francisco: Ignatius Press, 2005), 62–67.

everything from the destruction of church altar railings (so that everyone can see), to the exclusive reliance upon the vernacular (so that everyone can listen), to the call for women's ordination (so that everyone can consecrate). This is a misunderstanding. Rather than communicate a democratic impulse, what *participatio actuosa* urged was a deepening of the spirit of prayer.[51]

Grabbing hold again of the thread of our history, not every feature of the Liturgical Movement was unproblematic. In fact, parts of the eighteenth- and nineteenth-century liturgical renewal were less a reaction against the Enlightenment critique of revealed religion than a product of that critique. Some liturgists sought to rationalize the rites adapting them as though they were merely "instruction and moral admonition."[52] These wished to move Catholic liturgy closer to Protestant worship. Already in 1840 Guéranger cited twelve features of the growing anti-liturgical heresy that threatened to undermine authentic renewal of Catholic worship (cf. *Institutions liturgiques*, 1:408–414). These include: a false archaeological excavation of the past that seeks to "reproduce divine worship in its original purity" while disregarding later liturgical tradition (no. 4); the removing of ceremonies that leads to a loss of the mystical element of the liturgy (no. 5); the exclusion of the cult of the Blessed Virgin Mary and the saints (no. 7); the insistence of the use of the vernacular (no. 8); the desire to shorten the liturgy (no. 9); and the downplaying of the distinction between the priesthood of believers and the ministerial priesthood (no. 11).[53]

[51] See also Joseph Cardinal Ratzinger, *The Spirit of the Liturgy* (San Francisco: Ignatius Press, 200), 171–177 and SR 52.

[52] So the historical judgment of J. Jungmann, SJ, quoted by Reid, *The Organic Development of the Liturgy*, 53.

[53] Reid, *The Organic Development of the Liturgy*, 58–59.

Pope Pius XII's 1947 encyclical *Mediator Dei* and even the Second Vatican Council echoed many of these same concerns. For instance, Pius XII cautioned against "exaggerated and senseless antiquarianism" that had become attractive to some within the Liturgical Movement (MD 64). Liturgy could not be reconstructed simply from looking at the past. He warned against innovations in liturgical art. It would be disastrous, for one, to hang crucifixes "so designed that the divine Redeemer's body shows no trace of His cruel sufferings" (MD 63). In terms of language, he held up the use of Latin as "a manifest and beautiful sign of unity" in the Church (MD 59). With respect to piety, he encouraged devotion to the Sacred Heart of Jesus, to the Virgin Mother of God, as well as pilgrimages and similar traditional practices (MD 55).

Following this, the council's Constitution on the Sacred Liturgy (1962) taught that although other forms of music could be admitted, Gregorian chant was to retain "the pride of place" (SC 21); while it would be of advantage to allow for a greater use of the vernacular, especially in readings, prayers, and chants (SC 16), Latin was "to be retained in Catholic liturgies" (SC 24). Finally, although some adaptations were desirable, "there must be no innovations" unless absolutely required. The chief criterion for revision was to be as follows: "Any new forms adopted should in some way grow organically from forms already existing" (SC 23).

No doubt partly as a response to recent arbitrary innovations we find this principle articulated within the *Catechism* itself. Since liturgy is a constitutive element of holy living, "for this reason no sacramental rite may be modified or manipulated at the will of the minister or the community" (CCC 1125). Commenting on this text, Pope Benedict has called these "golden words" which "come from the depths of genuine liturgical understanding."[54]

Having restated many of the principles of the Liturgical Movement, *Sacrosanctum Concilium* did not present itself as an innovative document. Some have argued, nonetheless, that there is a gap between the council document and the liturgical texts that came out of it. Almost immediately after the liturgical commission began introducing texts of the new rite, alarms sounded. Some felt that what had been unleashed in the *Novus Ordo* was alien to the spirit and express intention of the liturgical reform movement.

Thus, in 1968 the Oratorian scholar Louis Bouyer (1913–2004), whose work had been influential at the council, wrote that under the pretext of "adapting" the liturgy, the liturgy had been destroyed:

> Perhaps in no other area is there as great a distance (and even a formal opposition) between what the Council worked out and what we actually have. Under the pretext of "adapting" the liturgy, people have simply forgotten that it is and can only be the traditional expression of the Christian mystery in all its spring-like fullness.[55]

Others found it particularly baneful that the priest should have to face the people. In a correspondence to Evelyn Waugh, Cardinal Heenan of Westminster speculated rather sardonically as to what this new turn in direction might mean. "The Mass is no longer the Holy Sacrifice but the meal at which the priest is

---

[54] Ratzinger, *On the Way to Jesus Christ*, 154.
[55] Louis Bouyer, *The Decomposition of Catholicism*, trans. C.U. Quinn (Chicago: Franciscan Herald Press, 1969), 105.

the waiter. The bishop, I suppose, is the Head Waiter and the Pope the Patron."[56]

These were not isolated protests. In 1988, in response to the dissatisfaction felt by many and in recognition of the twenty-fifth anniversary of *Sacrosantum Concilium*, Pope John Paul II issued the Apostolic Letter *Vicesimus Quintus Annus*. There he addressed some of the more egregious liturgical abuses that had become manifest. Apparently, a growing number of priests felt the need to be more responsive to their parishioners. In view of what were named as the pastoral needs of the people, some took to exercising creativity within the liturgy. John Paul II warned that "the right to compose Eucharistic prayers" and "to substitute profane readings" in place of Scripture did not belong to the authority of the priest (VQ 13). It did not belong to any individual, for that matter. Liturgical developments, he concluded, could proceed only as "the organic growth of a tree," which grows stronger "the deeper it sinks its roots into the soil of tradition" (VQ 23). Not only traditionalists have bemoaned this loss of reverence. More recently even the (former) Belgian primate Cardinal Daneels, an architect of the progressive movement within the Church since the 1960s, has acknowledged that liturgy has become an object of widespread clerical abuse. He has reflected how in the past rubrics dominated everything. "For want of being enlightened," priests formerly executed their actions with (in his view) a "puerile" obedience. The cardinal fears that today the reverse is the case: "It is the liturgy which

---

[56] John Carmel Cardinal Heenan, "Letter to Evelyn Waugh, August 28, 1964," in S.M.P. Reid, ed., *A Bitter Trial: Evelyn Waugh and Cardinal Heenan on the Liturgical Changes* (Curdridge: St. Austin Press, 1996), 48; cited in Rowland, *Ratzinger's Faith*, 138.

The Mass of St. Gregory, Israhel van Meckenem, German, c. 1490, engraving

must obey us and be adapted to our concerns, to the extent of becoming more like a political meeting or a 'happening.'"[57] That description, of course, does not fit every priest, or every liturgy. But it does describe the experience of many Catholics.

Just prior to his election Cardinal Ratzinger reflected on his own profound sense of disappointment at the subversion of the aims of the older Liturgical Movement. The movement that gave birth to the council's liturgical reform sought not to remove mystery from ritual but to heighten it, to offer it new breath. At its best, what the nineteenth- and early-twentieth century liturgists sought to overcome was a false reductionism, a false rationalism whereby ritual was simplified to an absolute minimum. In contrast the Liturgical Movement had emphasized that ritual developed within a living network of Tradition.

---

[57] Quoted in Fr. Jonathan Robinson, *The Mass and Modernity: Walking to Heaven Backward* (San Francisco: Ignatius Press, 2005), 31.

As Ratzinger wrote: "Anyone who, like me, was moved by this perception at the time of the Liturgical Movement on the eve of the Second Vatican Council can only stand, deeply sorrowing, before the ruins of the very things they were concerned for."[58]

Not only the words, but also the settings of worship have suffered. For reasons of pastoral concern or the desire to build community, liturgists throughout the 1970s and 1980s often uncritically adopted assumptions of modern philosophy and theories of art. First, instead of respecting the principle of the organic development of the liturgy, ritual was subject to sudden and dramatic alterations; and, as in the case of the priest's turn toward the people, changes were often founded upon dubious research. Second, as already mentioned, instead of promoting a deeper spirit of prayer, active participation heightened activity and lessened the distinction between the priesthood of the baptized and the priesthood of the ordained. These disruptions in cult, it seems, go some distance toward explaining why worship has become less interesting for Catholics.

Consider the loss of Latin. Instead of uniting us to the past, and so giving us a vantage for judging the future, a wholly vernacular liturgy sounds a lot like everyday speech. It becomes more parochial. Instead of uniting us to the words and syllables spoken on the lips of St. Augustine and St. John of the Cross, St. Thomas More and St. Thérèse of Lisieux, our prayers sound like the conversation at the office; it also lessens our communion with believers who speak foreign languages. If we use everyday language, we should not be surprised when ritual becomes mundane. Neither modern popes nor recent councils have called

[58] See Ratzinger's preface to Reid's *Organic Development of the Liturgy*, 11.

for an end to Latin. Indeed, in the year that Blessed John XXIII opened Vatican II, he published a dispassionate plea for the rejuvenation of the Church's common tongue. His Apostolic Constitution *Veterum Sapientia* (1962) cites three benefits for the Church: Latin unifies. Latin stabilizes. Latin elevates. "For the Church, precisely because it embraces all nations and is destined to endure to the end of time ... requires a language which is universal, immutable, and non-vernacular."

Alongside the loss of the sense of the organic development of the liturgy, and of the proper dispositions of laypersons, we can mention one other. Many of us have forgotten why Catholics worship at all. We have forgotten not only the sacrificial nature of the Mass but also how the Mass relates to the soup kitchen. Hence, a third false conclusion about liturgy: the tacit assumption that good works or instruction are more valuable than ritual. With the shift, particularly to the latter, the priest's role tends to grow exponentially. Undoubtedly the casual approach of many priests to the liturgy has made the modern Church less dynamic. If you no longer see yourself as the servant of a tradition but its master, no longer believe that the rubrics veil a mystery, that the soul requires truth to be wrapped in the garment of beauty, then reasonably you are likely to treat the Mass more as a gathering of friends than as a sacrifice of God. Others catch on. Most move on. And insofar as liturgy is mined for alien purposes, its capacity to excite as the source and summit of our salvation diminishes.

The story has not ended there, of course. For those communities and individuals that have remained attached to the older forms of Catholic liturgical piety—or are discovering them anew—the pontificate of Benedict XVI has offered great encouragement. For a start, in most dioceses the worst of the liturgical experimentations appear to be over. In a growing number of parishes the *Novus Ordo* is said with faithful attention to the prescribed forms as set forth in the *General Instruction of the Roman Missal*. The International Committee on English in the Liturgy (ICEL) has delivered an improved translation of the ordinary form of the Mass.[59] Additionally, if Benedict XVI's influence will be felt by young priests and seminarians, it will not be long before parishioners once again expect their clergy to read Latin and sing Gregorian chant.[60] And since the Holy Father's 2007 *Motu Proprio, Summorum Pontificum*, there are no longer any canonical restrictions on Catholics who wish to celebrate Mass according to the 1962 Missal. That is to say, there remain only practical restrictions. Even though the Tridentine Mass has been restored and given once again "due honor for its

[59] The improvements exhibited within the new translation are, chiefly, threefold: a preference for a more elevated over a colloquial style (e.g., *Et cum spiritu tuo*, from "And also with you" is now, "And with your spirit"); a more accurate rendering of the text itself (e.g., the three-fold repetition *Mea culpa, mea culpa, mea maxima culpa* is preserved, as opposed to, formerly, the single line, "through my own fault"); the new translation is more faithful to the theological nuances present in the original (e.g., *Agnus Dei qui tollis peccata mundi*, is now "Lamb of God, you take away the sins [peccata] of the world" as opposed to, in the old version, merely sin—in the singular—which presumably intended to minimize the individual character of sin in favor of its collective nature. See the early comment on ICEL's revision given by Michael Gilchrist, "New Improved English Mass Translation Nears Completion," in *AD2000* 17, no. 6 (July 2004):3.

[60] As in *Sacramentum Caritatis*, his Post Synodal Exhortation on the Eucharist: "Speaking more generally, I ask that future priests, from their time in seminary, receive the preparation needed to understand and to celebrate Mass in Latin, and also to use Latin texts and execute Gregorian chant" (SR 62).

venerable and ancient usage" (SP art. 1), finding a willing and able priest remains a barrier. Still, as the number of young people who wish to worship according to the extraordinary form of the Latin rite increases, as is particularly the case among university students, so too will access to it.

Liturgical disputes can sometimes appear like political conflicts. They need not take this form. In what remains I wish to explore the biblical foundations for Catholic liturgy. By looking at the history of the Jewish cult, I hope to make clear why the *Catechism* regards not social service, not evangelism, but worship as the Church's most important work. For, according to the *Catechism*, when priests (and laity for that matter) set aside the forms of the liturgy, they not only display a lack of reverence; they undermine the revealed blueprint for the Church's mission. It is for this reason that among the most urgent tasks in the renewal of Catholic culture is what the Dominican theologian Fr. Aidan Nichols has called the "re-enchantment of the liturgy."[61]

Liturgy in the mission of the Church

With some of the recent history of liturgical practice and theory in view, we are in a better position to consider why the Church takes liturgy to be at the heart of her mission. It will be useful to begin with a definition. In the ancient world a liturgy (*leitourgia*) was a public work, usually performed by a wealthy citizen on behalf of the community. So, for instance, when Athens prepared for war, rich citizens had to outfit the battleships. A *leitourgia* may also include the sponsoring of a dramatic

---

[61] Aidan Nichols, *Christendom Awake* (Grand Rapids: William B. Eerdmans, 1999), 21.

festival, the production of a chorus, or of an athletic team.[62] In Christian usage this basic sense is retained and given a precise application. A liturgy is still a public service. Now, however, God is the primary actor. Sometimes you will hear it said that liturgy is the "work of the people." This is a misunderstanding. It is the *totus Christus* (the whole Christ) which acts in liturgy. The work of the Body is wholly dependent upon the work of Christ, our Head. According to the *Catechism*, liturgy is "the participation of the People of God in the 'work of God'"; and, through liturgy "Christ, our redeemer and high priest, continues the work of our redemption in, with, and through his Church" (CCC 1069). Christ is the primary actor, although he acts with us and through us.

In Christian usage, we might say that liturgy retains the form of the classical definition, as a work of the people, but the meaning of those words is inverted. We do not perform a service because we are witty, wealthy, or wise. Unlike in the classical sense, the work is Christ's, and our personal initiative is not required. This is why, in relation to the misapplied understanding of *active participation*, as Cardinal, Ratzinger has emphasized that it is not external action that the council called for but a greater spiritual attention to the action *of* God in the Mass. "The real 'action' in the liturgy in which we are all supposed to participate is the action of God himself."[63] As Pope, Benedict XVI has reiterated the same: "It should be made clear that the word 'participation' does not refer to mere external activity during the celebration" (SR 52). We share in the work of God but

[62] "Liturgy" in the *Oxford Classical Dictionary*, 3rd ed., eds. S. Hornblower and A. Spawforth (Oxford: Oxford University Press, 1996).

[63] Ratzinger, *The Spirit of the Liturgy*, 173.

in the way that a string shares in the flight of a kite, or in the way that a glove shares in the work of a hand. We do not take the lead. We are not asked to be creative. Our will must will to conform; there are genuflections to make and chants to sing. We can consent to be pulled by the twitch of the finger or the toss of the wind, but we cannot generate these motions. Our part in the opus Dei is essential, but it is secondary.

There is another feature to the definition of *liturgy*. We already saw that Christ works "in, with, and through his Church." Further on we discover that this presence is manifest in some activities more than others. There exist degrees of presence. A friend is certainly present to you on your birthday when he sends a gift in the mail. After you open the card, see his script, and read his words, you smile. But that presence can intensify. Once John and Judy crash through your front door, sit down at your table, and eat your cake, then you will laugh. The body makes a difference.

Like some noisy friend, God is forever banging on our door. He gave us birth and then sent us an invitation to the birthday party of his Son. But as every host knows, celebration requires preparation; in this case it took a few thousand years to complete. The history of Jewish cult is the record of God's setting the table, preparing the world for the vast feast that all the nations would attend. The ceremonial codes regulating Jewish worship told the people in a hundred ways that there were hot points, peaks along the vast and lonely plains where they might look for God in the desert of this life. As we know, once the Jews finally did arrive in Jerusalem, one site was set apart, the Temple. Its inner precincts became, as it were, the rod that God established amid the Jews so that they would have some way of anticipating when and where the lightning would strike.

The Golden Gate, Jerusalem

In the transition between the two covenants, Jesus' body replaces the Temple. Few at his death understood the meaning of Christ's words. As George Herbert imagines Christ to say,

> *Some said, that I the Temple to the floore*
> *In three dayes raz'd, and raised as before.*
> *Why, he that built the world can do much more*
> — "The Sacrifice," in *The Temple* (1633)

Christ is that conducting point. According to the traditional formula, once a person is baptized, he shares in the triple "offices" of Christ. The offices describe the means by which we participate in the divine life; they point to the threefold manner by which Jesus Christ fulfilled the Jews' messianic expectations; and they are essential to understanding the purpose of liturgy.

The three offices are prefigured by the three modes of mediation in the Old Testament. First, God established the ministry of priesthood. This office or ministry was the means by which satisfaction and atonement for sin could be made. Everything about the priestly ministry — the times, the places, the material, and the manner of sacrifices — is revealed by God and legislated for the people (cf. Lev. 16). The sacrificial system was integral to Israel's Law. The Law taught the Jews how to gather light and heat from the fire without being consumed, how to live in the midst of a holy God. Remember too that *Torah* (which designates the five books revealed through Moses) means above all "the way of life." What God revealed on Mount Sinai was how his people were to approach God; conduct followed cult. If you are to be a holy people, you must do *this* and not do *that*. God reveals ethics so that the people can properly worship. You need only think of the structure of the Ten Commandments: by design the laws that regulate society come after the laws that satisfy God (Exod. 20:1–17). In the Old and New Testaments, cult comes first, then community.

The second mode by which God mediated his presence was by the ministry of the prophets. Unlike the priestly caste — which all came from the Levites — you never knew where a prophet might arise. They appear in unexpected circumstances, in the midst of humiliating exile (as Jeremiah did during the Babylonian captivity [Jer. 29]); or knocking on the king's door (as Nathan did at King David's palace [2 Sam. 12]); or speaking out of the lips of an ass (as Balaam discovered [Num. 22]). They might wander in the desert or disappear in an explosion of fire; they might foretell judgment or promise mercy, but what is common to the prophets is this: with one voice they preached fidelity to the Law. God would be faithful to his promises, if only his people would remain faithful to theirs. There is development in Israel's understanding of the meaning of the Torah, certainly, but the prophets are forever at its service, threatening, warning, pleading, so that the people might come back to the covenant.

Third is the ministry of the kings. It was under doubtful circumstances that the Lord allowed Israel to have a king at all. The people, we are told, wished to have a king "so that they might be like the other nations" (cf. 1 Sam. 8:5–18). God allowed them a king as a concession. Then, bringing good out of evil, the prophets began to foretell that God would send to the people a king who would also be a savior. The anointed one, this "Christ," would be a king of the line of David, although one superior to him. In other words, a growing expectation developed in the last centuries before Christ that not only would God send a king, but that the king would rule and serve like no other king. Somehow, God would make an appearance. He would arrive, as Isaiah said, as Emmanuel, God with us (cf. Matt. 1:23; Isa. 7:14).

Now, the first disciples believed that Christ was this savior. They believed that in his own person Jesus fulfilled the hopes of the Old Testament: all the expectation the Jews had for a more intimate communion with God, for a more complete fidelity to the Law, and for a more perfect ruler. When Christ told the Jews that before Abraham was born "I am" (John 8:58) he knew, as they also knew, precisely what he was saying. "I am who I am" is the name God revealed to Moses at the burning bush, on Mount Sinai (Exod. 3:14). By adopting that title, Jesus identified himself with God's very self, and that is why the Jews called him a blasphemer. What Christ was saying was not merely that he mediated God's presence, not merely that he taught God's word, not merely that he ruled by divine authority, but that he was all these things combined: he was the expected priest, the expected prophet, and the expected king. Jesus in his person literally was *God with us* to a degree that stretched beyond the imagination of some of the Jews; and so they hung him on the Cross.

Why does any of this history matter? It matters because God's way with the Jews established certain lines of communication that would be continued in the age of the Church. When the Church teaches, therefore, that Jesus fulfilled the triple offices of priest, prophet, and king, following on from the Old Testament, it asserts that he mediates God's presence in a maximal way. Now, I think, we can answer why the Church elevates liturgy among her ministries. The pattern of God's redemptive activity did not alter between the covenants. The triple offices of the Old Testament correspond to the three ministries within the Church. In worship the Church performs the priestly office; in proclamation, the prophetic; and in service, the kingly (CCC 1070, 1072).

Given this theological trajectory, it is clear that each office is essential to the Church. You could hardly imagine that prayer was all that was required of Catholics, any more than you could think that you had only to read books or serve at a soup kitchen. Each work is necessary. Still, there is an order. Herein lies a clue, I think, as to why much of contemporary Catholicism has lost its power over culture. We often fail to discriminate between the *types* of presence. God is indeed everywhere present; but he is not present everywhere in the same manner or to the same degree. And as it happens, he has taught us where we will maximally find his power acting in the world. There exists an objective ordering among the ministries of the Church. As the *Catechism* relates, it is in the Church's priestly service that Christ acts most "efficaciously" and "in the highest degree."

This is traditional Catholic teaching. Lest anyone imagine it is antiquated, we note that the doctrine was expressed also at the council. The *Catechism* quotes at length from the Second Vatican Council's Constitution on the Sacred Liturgy:

> The liturgy then is rightly seen as an exercise of the priestly office of Jesus Christ. It involves the presentation of man's sanctification under the guise of signs perceptible by the senses and its accomplishment in ways appropriate to each of these signs. In it full public worship is performed by the Mystical Body of Jesus Christ, that is, by the Head and his members. From this it follows that every liturgical celebration, because it is an action of Christ the priest and of his Body which is the Church, is a sacred action surpassing all others. *No other action of the Church can equal its efficacy by the same title and to the same degree.* (CCC 1070; quoting SC 7.2–3; *emphasis mine*)

Liturgy is an exercise of the priestly office of Christ, and it is through worship that Christ (through the Church) acts most powerfully in the world. We began by posing the question: Why do so many Catholics stay in bed on Sundays? Here is one answer: having permitted indifference to rubrics, having perpetuated a new clericalism, having promoted a misguided activism, we have deployed the liturgy for alien purposes and now too often reap what some have sown. Since liturgy forms faith and is God's favored means of dispensing grace, every act of disregard for the liturgy is an insult to or, rather, an assault upon the faith. The primary role that liturgy has in forming character and communicating God's grace is one reason Benedict XVI has dedicated much of his pontificate to restoring dignity in our corporate worship. The Church cares about sharing, but giving to charities is evidently not a Catholic's highest act of worship.

Here we have spoken about the deficit in our understanding of liturgy; in the next chapter we speak about the deficit in our presentation. Our task will be to consider the sacramental vision of Catholicism, and to explore how it is that the soul can rise to God through signs and symbolic representation, by the sacraments and through Christian art.

The Baptism of Christ, Italian, c. 1340, tempera on panel

4

On Sacraments:
When the World Is Enchanted

A good evangelist is clever as well as forceful. You need to be sharp to discover obstacles and blunt to overcome them. Advertisers understand this well. Coca-Cola annually spends three billion dollars selling sugar water. Most of that budget is directed toward children eight to twelve years old. There is good reason for this. Between these ages the young are most vulnerable to suggestion and least inhibited to spend. Symbols sell. Corporations want their logos to be seen because these create an association between our desires and their products. Bishops, of course, cannot compete with big business. Yet there remains one respect in which the preacher has an advantage over our corporate masters. Coca-Cola must create a need; the Church need only satisfy one.

We are born with infinite appetite. As St. Augustine said, our hearts are restless. They are indeed, but our true needs can remain unnamed and unnoticed amid so much noisy competition. We are forever hunting, therefore, but for what, it can be difficult to say. The young girl wandering through the mall, the young man trapped by images on his computer screen, are both in their own way looking for a way back to Eden. Thorns cover the path. Can we return? Through liturgy we can at least make a beginning. Catholic worship offers a glimpse of Heaven; as history has shown, merely a look can be enough to remake the earth.

In the last chapter, we spoke of the deficit in our understanding of liturgy, and especially of the meaning of active participation. Here we speak of the deficit in presentation. Our reflections will proceed in three stages. We take up first the evangelizing power of beauty; then, how worship must be enchanted; lastly, we will apply these insights to the practice of the sacred arts, the building of churches.

Beauty and evangelization

Created realities attract because they first reflect. Through them we catch glimpses of another country, like the dance of light shimmering upon a lake on the far side of a forest. The world charms, indeed; but we are ever bumping into a beauty that points us beyond the world. The atheist, shielded by his ideas, must be careful where he steps. Every field for him is a minefield, as Wordsworth says,

Wivenhoe Park, Essex, John Constable

On Sacraments

Hence in a season of calm weather
Though inland far we be
Our Souls have sight of that immortal sea
Which brought us hither,
Can in a moment travel thither,
And see the Children sport upon the shore,
And hear the mighty waters rolling evermore.

("Ode: Intimations of Immortality," 161–167)

These glimpses are given by design. When we catch sight of glory in creatures, we do really see something of the true, something of the good, and something of the beautiful shining through them. Creatures attract because they have a likeness to God. From apples to angels, everything reflects, in some way, divine truth, goodness, and beauty.[64] Since everything that exists comes from the good God, to exist is to be good.

This is why evil, in the Catholic tradition, is not a substance. Evil is not a *thing*; it is only a negation. The Devil cannot create. He can only act, and act as it were on the purely spiritual plain by prompts and suggestions. Upon human beings he works by tricking us into loving good things in bad ways, as Eve did with the apple, as Augustine did with the pears (cf. *Confessions*, 2.4.9.). After his theft Augustine tossed the fruit, not because he thought his neighbor's farming practices were unkind to the earth, but for the more lofty motive of wanting to be loved by his friends. And so we stalk on. The heart, like some lonely wolf, trots across the vast and barren plains of our nights and days looking for God, scratching under every shiny stone.

---

[64] On this see entry "Transcendentals" in the *New Catholic Encyclopedia*, 2nd edition.

Three of the traditional transcendentals—the good, the true, and the beautiful—reflect aspects of the one reality of who God is. In the order of reality, the transcendentals are unified in God. God's mode of being is good, true, and beautiful. In us, this unity is present but not always apparent. We often experience one of these characteristics more keenly than another. Some among us are moved more by argument than by affection; others more by beauty than by debate. Temperament and circumstance will largely dictate such preferences. Where education has not yet devolved into careerism, one of the chief aims of a liberal education is to help you discover which of the transcendentals moves you most: goodness, truth, or beauty. We can take this basic psychological insight a step further. Not only individuals are attracted by this trio; whole cultures are too and can likewise display a preference. So, which is most appealing to us postmoderns? Arguably, in our day appeal to the true and the good are frustrated in a way that appeal to beauty is not. Our skepticism and our cynicism have left many in our culture cold to the apologist and even to the missionary of charity, but not to the artist.

By way of illustration, take the appeal to truth. Among the evils of relativism, the view that "knowledge" is only a cloak for opinion and that propositions cannot travel across time and place is the way that it prematurely closes debate. It often does this quite literally. I could offer a dozen examples. Here are two.

In English-speaking countries university students are usually governed by student unions. These organizations, which represent students before faculty and administration, are notoriously run by the most radical elements of the student population. Often they work to ensure conformity to whatever politically correct doctrine happens to be blowing across campus. Of all the orthodoxies at universities these days, matters of sexual license are most hallowed. Students learn fast that at university you are free to air the most outrageous criticisms. You may ridicule your government, your religion, your history, even your own mother, but never shall a word be spoken against free sex! One of the more humorous instances of thought-policing was in a series of posters I recently came across at a public university at which I was speaking. Throughout this otherwise lovely campus, the visitor's eye was caught by a series of signs posted by the student union which displayed the following warning: "This is a safe place!" What could it all mean? Did the cafeteria finally rid its refrigerators of E. coli? Were the lab mice recovered? Then I noticed a rainbow symbol, and my fears were assuaged. The signs referred not to the safe cafeteria or to the clean labs, but to the metaphorical "space," as in the space between the students' ears, the space of speech. Thus, when you enter a "safe space" the student union's welcome committee had promised that nothing offensive will be heard. There is no little irony here. In the early modern phase of the West's experiment with political liberalism, the principle of freedom of speech was most vigorously defended by those who identified with revolutionary politics. So Voltaire (1694–1778) in the 1760s could voice a sentiment that held even into the 1960s: "I disapprove of what you say, but I will defend to the death your right to say it." Roles have reversed. Today social conservatives defend free speech while the far left tries to bury it.

I pull a second example from the national news. Recently Ann Coulter, an American conservative and author of seven *New York Times* bestselling books, traveled to the University of Ottawa to give a public address. Prior to her arrival, the university administration issued a not-so-subtle threat that Coulter risked legal repercussions if she spoke in Canada as she does in the United States. The message was clear: tone down or stay home. Not cowed, Coulter arrived as scheduled. So did a lot of others. Large crowds had gathered, some to show support, others their displeasure. But Coulter never delivered her talk. As was widely reported, instead of being forced to do battle from behind the podium, she was sent fleeing under armed guard. From the television interviews that followed after the debacle, the small group of students responsible for the protest were elated. When a reporter asked the women in charge whether she saw a contradiction in the resort to physical violence to stop what she considered "violent speech," the poor student simply repeated that the speaker was a threat to the peace.[65] What are we to make of this? Now, some might find Ms. Coulter rude or even silly, but she is not a threat in any legally relevant sense.

Forceful argument and violent force are not equivalent. In civilized jurisdictions, laws protect against language that portends material harm. For instance, when a man grimaces and says, "I am going to punch your nose," you take an interest in those words; so does the law. When he declares his intention to visit the "space" between your eyes with his knuckles you not unreasonably begin to feel unsafe. That poses a rather different sort of threat, however, from that of someone who earns her butter poking fun at you and your ideas.

Earlier in the liberal tradition, openness to free speech had been regarded as a necessary condition for the discovery of truth. Embedded within the West's doctrine of political liberalism is the largely Christian faith in the rationality of speech and

---

[65] On the debacle see further Mark Steyn's comments in "True North Strong and Free," in *Maclean's*, April 12, 2010, 24–26.

of the possibility of conversion through persuasive argument.[66] That faith has largely failed. And we should not be surprised that it has. Once truth vanishes, so too does the motivation to search. As a consequence, increasingly we live under the watch of those who police the mind.

The principle that the above two anecdotes illustrate is this: skepticism is not a condition of dialogue, but its end. If all opinions are equal, then all are quite equally untrue. In such a climate, conflicts in opinion inevitably are reduced to conflicts of will, and hence of force. An agnostic might make a respectable case that four hundred years ago, religious institutions were heavy-handed in their treatment of dissenters. But Elizabethan England, like the European Wars of Religion, is a distant memory. In our century it was secular fundamentalism (Facist and Socialist) that posed the greatest threat to freedom of thought. Today not religious creeds but liberal dogmas most hinder intellectual freedom. Progressive education is that form of instruction that begins from the premise of skeptical materialism. This sort of learning, far from freeing students, only inoculates them against being capable to feel the most ennobling of passions: the pleasure of discovery and the pain of contradiction. So much loss for so little gain. The relativist, in supposing that he must sacrifice his instinct for truth in exchange for amicability, turns out, in the end, to be open and to be tolerant only in the most insipid of ways. He is open, but only to the degree that he remains closed to argument; he is tolerant, but only so long as he speaks with someone who shares his nonbelief. Should you challenge this modern knight to a duel, or bang on the door of his castle with the hammer of reason, should you, in

[66] On this see Oliver O'Donovan, *The Desire of the Nations* (Cambridge: Cambridge University Press, 1997), 268–271.

other words, challenge his premises, question his inferences, or suggest inconsistencies among his conclusions, far from laying down his sword, your adversary will simply raise his last defense. He wears his armor with pride. You will see painted across his shield not the wild symbols of the Celts, not the fleur-de-lis of the Christians, but only a scribbled message in black ink: *That's your opinion*. With this, the battle is won. Without flag, without ceremony, desire for truth, the four-thousand-year-old history of philosophy that winds from Egypt to Athens to America, the tightened bow of man's will to knowledge, is undone. Each one goes his way "free," as we say, "to disagree." On our university campuses, the novels of Sartre and Camus now look as dated as bell-bottoms and flower-patterned skirts. Modern man

Self-Portrait, Vincent van Gogh, Dutch, 1889, oil on canvas

dies not in a final ecstasy of rebellion, but merely suffocating in the intellectual prison of his own self-imposed solitary confinement, whimpering. Or, if you are a postmodern undergraduate, you might yell at Ann Coulter.

We should not exaggerate. Reason still revolts against unreason. It is the Catholic conviction that nothing can ever fully extinguish the desire for truth (or for goodness, for that matter). My point is only that in an age of relativism, the apologist for truth, as the laborer for justice, faces a thousand obstacles. For the artist, it is quite different. He still has a receptive audience. My guess is that few atheists have thumbed through the *Catechism*. But everyone has read *The Lord of the Rings*, which in 1999 was ranked in an international survey as the "greatest novel of the century."[67] Tolkien called the work a Catholic epic.[68] I have no idea how many people Frodo has brought to Christ; but surely the beauty of Tolkien's art has nudged millions of readers closer to the Catholic view of Heaven.[69] Unlike the philosopher's pen, the artist's paint, stone, and melody penetrate where naked argument cannot enter. Not that truth and beauty conflict. As the great nineteenth-century evangelist

[67] By Amazon.com; also a 2003 BBC survey found that *The Lord of the Rings* was England's most beloved novel.

[68] Tolkien once remarked to a family friend Fr. Robert Murray, SJ, "The Lord of the Rings is of course a fundamentally religious and Catholic work; unconsciously so at first, but consciously in the revision. That is why I have not put in, or have cut out, practically all references to anything like 'religion', to cults or practices, in the imaginary world. For the religious element is absorbed into the story and the symbolism" (Letter no. 142) in *The Letters of J.R.R. Tolkien*, ed. H. Carpenter with C. Tolkien (London: Allen and Unwin, 1981), 172.

[69] See, for instance, the study by Joseph Pearce, *Tolkien: Man and Myth* (San Francisco: Ignatius Press, 1998).

and refounder of the French Dominicans, Fr. Henri-Dominique Lacordaire (1802–1861) has said, "Truth has a vesture, a halo ... beauty."[70] When beauty fails, when the arts flounder, truth is soon to be forgotten. We might ask: How does this relate to our presentation of the liturgy? It relates directly. Ritual renders truth intelligible to a religiously illiterate people. Damage ritual, and you destroy faith.

A familiar historical anecdote illustrates well the evangelizing power of beauty. After his brother's death in 980, Vladimir became the ruler of Kiev, whose people were descendants of Norse chiefs and traders. Although Sts. Cyril and Methodius had converted many of the Slavs a century before, the rulers largely remained pagan. As the *Primary Russian Chronicle* relates, Vladimir's father had been fiercely attached to pagan customs. Once in power Vladimir likewise attempted to revitalize the old rites in his realm. The attempt failed. It is said that when the prince recognized the recalcitrance of his people, he accepted at the same time the need to embrace a monotheistic religion. But which one? To help him decide, in 987 he sent a troupe on a world study tour. Their task: visit the neighboring nations, watch, and report how they worship. When the men returned they explained to their prince that they had found the true faith. The company related to Vladimir their experience of the worship of the divine liturgy of St. John Chrysostom:

> Then we went to Greece, and the Greeks led us to the edifices where they worship their God, and we knew not whether we were in heaven or on earth. For on earth

---

[70] Fr. Henri-Dominique Lacordaire, *Life: Conferences Delivered at Toulouse*, trans. T. D. Langdon (New York: P. O'Shea Publishers, 1874), 190.

there is no such splendor or such beauty, and we are at a loss to describe it. We only know that God dwells there among men, and their service is fairer than the ceremonies of other nations. For we cannot forget that beauty.[71]

Largely on the testimony of this report Vladimir adopted the faith in 988, the year that Eastern Europeans cite as the establishment of Christianity in their region. But note this: despite the evangelizing power of beauty within the liturgy, this is not yet its first function. Its primary purpose is, as we might say, disinterested. Foremost it functions to render glory unto God. Only as an afterthought does it become useful for the building up of God's people.

The enchantment of the liturgy

So beauty elevates and beauty transforms. The best catechesis on the liturgy is, of course, the liturgy itself, celebrated well. If liturgy is to have its full effect in shaping culture it must regain once more its power to *enchant*. As Pope Benedict has recently explained, beauty is not mere decoration within liturgy, "but rather an essential element" (SR 35). How can we bring beauty back into our sacramental worship? Seven in number, the sacraments are efficacious signs (CCC 1210, 1131). Although all of them are essential to the Christian life, they are ordered in rank to the Eucharist "as to their end" (CCC 1211). The sacraments do not depend on our understanding, although they are aided by it (cf. CCC 1253). Being at once body and spirit, "man expresses and perceives spiritual realities through physical signs

---

[71] *Russian Primary Chronicle*, trans. and ed. S. H. Cross and O. P. Sherbowitz-Wetzor (Cambridge, Massachusetts: The Medieval Academy of America, 1953), 111.

and symbols" (CCC 1146). Some ages may have forgotten that sacraments are efficacious; ours seems not to remember that they are also *signs*.[72] Grace builds upon nature. The sensuous nature of the sacraments—their clothing, we might even say— is not incidental. In part, the medium is the message.

Good liturgy is enchanted. What do we mean by this? To what do we aspire when we hope to re-enchant our worship? According to one rendering of its etymology, *to enchant* (Latin: *in cantare*) literally means to sing something into being. Thus, when Catholics say that the world is enchanted, they mean this: that creation, far from stumbling into an accidental existence, was sung into being by the voice of her maker. The world is alive by design. Nature throws God's voice back at us like some mighty echo heard roaring against a canyon wall, sometimes indistinct but never mistakable. Almost immediately after the Enlightenment had proclaimed the reign of a godless science, there arose defenders of an enchanted nature, the nature replete with purposes. What the Romantic poets and latterly some of our scientists have tried to recover is the ancient conviction that the world is charged with the grandeur of God. Among recent authors there is the poetry of Gerard Manley Hopkins, SJ (1844–1889), the epics of J.R.R. Tolkien (1892–1973), and the allegories of C.S. Lewis (1898–1963). Who could forget that remarkable moment in *The Magician's Nephew*, for instance, when Aslan literally *sings* Narnia into

---

[72] Interior participation, or true active participation in the Mass, requires formation in three elements, only one of which do we focus on here. As specified in *Sacramentum Caritatis*, these three are: 1) interpreting the rites in the light of salvation history; 2) presenting the meaning of the signs; 3) explaining their significance for Christian life (cf. SR 64).

being.[73] The children watch in wonder as the great lion, with the voice of ten thousand horns, calls forth the stars and the planets and the trees of his new world.

> It was so beautiful he [the boy, Digory] could hardly bear it.... The lion was pacing to and fro about that empty land and singing his new song. It was softer and more lilting than the song by which he had called up the stars and the sun; a gentle, rippling music. And as he walked and sang the valley grew green with grass.[74]

For liturgy and the sacraments to make sense to us, Narnia must be a real place. It is a country not only for children. For matter to communicate, nature in our world too must in *some sense* be alive, must be capable of communicating intention, of throwing back an echo. To overcome the deficit in our presentation of liturgy we must believe again, understand again, recover again the older vision of creation—and by extension, artistic creation—as the song of God.

Consider the alternative. If matter were merely dull, if rock and wood, and along with them glass and pigment, were no more than what geologists weigh and chemists measure, then nature could not speak, because there would be nothing for her to say. Our world of bread and water, wine and oil must be alive if indeed it is through such common offerings that God pours forth his grace. In short, the enchanted liturgy is liturgy that, by

---

[73] My thanks to Joseph Pearce and his reflections on C. S. Lewis's *Narnia* at the 2010 Western Canadian Catholic Homeschooling Conference in Edmonton, Alberta, which I have drawn upon here.

[74] C. S. Lewis, *The Magician's Nephew* (New York: Harper Trophy, 2000), 106, 112.

means of created signs, pulls back the veil of the temple to offer us a glimpse of the transcendent. Faithfully rendered, artistic mastery over the signs and symbols of the sacraments carries us over to the glory of the Lord. As with the conversion of the Slavs, cult retains its power to produce culture, a total system of life transformed by the Gospel.

We have said, then, that Christian worship assumes that creation itself is a revelation. Reason is fitted to read nature. The theory and practice of sacramental worship presupposes that nature symbolizes, and thus can communicate, something of the divine. The *Catechism* reiterates this traditional view.

> God speaks to man through the visible creation. The material cosmos is so presented to man's intelligence that he can read there traces of its Creator. Light and darkness, wind and fire, water and earth, the tree and its fruit speak of God and symbolize both his greatness and his nearness. (CCC 1147)

Nature is alive, in other words, insofar as it expresses *intentions*. Grace presupposes nature. So too liturgy, and indeed every artistic production, presupposes a world of natural (and cultural) symbolism. In the Catholic view, art always includes the imitation of nature. But once man becomes separated from nature, or begins to suppose nature to be unresponsive to his reason, his artistic productions likewise will lose their rational character. Man's art, instead of expressing order, becomes arbitrary. It loses definiteness of form. It reflects back not a cosmos but merely a chaos. This is why flipping through a book of expressionist paintings or walking through the Tate Modern Gallery in London can sometimes have the feel of stepping into a nightmare. I do not deny that there is a public willing to pay for horror. The term *creativity* in its modern usage is a concept born of the Marxist worldview. Creativity in a godless world is the sheer assertion of will in a meaningless universe, a universe without purpose, without direction, without beauty.[75] We should be clear about the ideas behind the images. It is no coincidence that the age that produced Jean Paul Sartre is the same period that saluted Jackson Pollock's splattered paint and sat quietly listening while John Cage dropped pianos. Rage and Stoic resignation are the only positions left open for the artist who cannot or will not see the hand of the Creator behind his own creations.

Nor should Christians leave questions of art only to so-called experts. Beauty is essential to our worship; given the august tradition of Western art, beauty is, after all, what Catholics used to know most about. So, since the Church employs the arts for her worship, she can be neither indifferent nor diffident when it comes to competing accounts of aesthetics. Defenders of modernist art usually claim freedom has been given a new lease. Being liberated from actual objects, the artist was supposedly empowered to exercise an expanded freedom, so the claim went.[76] In reality, the opposite happened. The rise of abstractionism in art is not a sign of vital creativity; it is a sign of its decay. All freedom depends upon some limit. Nowhere is this

---

[75] On this see Ratzinger's prescient comments in *The Spirit of the Liturgy*, 168.

[76] The famous Marxist art critic Harold Rosenberg (1906–1978) described accurately, and approvingly, the mood of leading artists after the Second World War as follows: "The lone artists did not want the world to be different, he wanted his canvas to be a world. Liberation from the object meant liberation from 'nature,' society and art already there," in *The Tradition and the Now* [1959] (New York: Da Capo Press, 1996), 30.

more evident than in the fine arts. Works of art cannot even ape existence (the way ideas sometimes can) apart from their instantiation in some definite, concrete, and thus limited, form; both the archetypal forms and the matter for human creations are received first as gifts. Human creativity is in this way always derivative. As John Paul II remarked in his *Letter to Artists*:

> With loving regard, the divine Artist passes on to the human artist a spark of surpassing wisdom, calling him or her to share in divine creative power. Obviously, this is a sharing that leaves intact the infinite distance between the Creator and the creature, as Cardinal Nicholas of Cusa made clear: "Creative art, which it is the soul's good fortune to entertain, is not to be identified with that essential art, which is God himself, but is only a communication of it and a share in it." (LA 1)

In eschewing nature as a norm for his work the Impressionist or the Abstract Expressionist or the Surrealist must substitute some other measure—invariably, himself. Art becomes auto-biography, or worse, publically financed therapy. Has it ever struck you why the explanations that accompany most mod-ernist works are so dreary, and so long? The reason is this: It is no longer the work that communicates about the world open to common experience—after all, that is not the point—but the artist sharing himself. Let us not be misled. Picasso was just David Hume with a brush between his teeth, skepticism splashed with color. For the modernists, perception of form no longer matters because the world, like some ball of sand, has already slipped between his fingers.

Here as elsewhere responsible catechesis will not only have to proclaim the truth but also name what has gone wrong. If our

artistic productions are once more to fulfill their highest function—that of rendering glory to God—and also of drawing
people to faith, we will not only have to renew a sacramental
view of creation; we will also have to recover the artistic skills
and imagination suitable to such a view.[77] In what remains, our
final task will be to try to make concrete the *Catechism's* sacramental vision by turning to one kind of ecclesiastical art in particular: church architecture. Renewing our houses of worship
will require many things; at the least it will mean taking them
back from architects who have been trained in the schools of
modern philosophy.

Modern art and sacred architecture

Oscar Wilde once quipped that only a shallow person does
not judge by appearances. He is, of course, mostly right. We
cannot but judge by what we see. The beautiful face of a sleep-
ing child evokes wonder. My wife and I make a point of peek-
ing in at our five little boys each night before we fall into bed.
Somehow, at the sight of them, so still, so peaceful, so quiet,
all offenses are forgotten, all sacrifices rewarded. The surface
counts. It is not as though seeing your son's red cheek is a prelude to some deeper anatomical study. A strict materialist might
well call parents Romantic, and he would be right; but that does
not mean they are unrealistic or unscientific. The materialist
must say that bones, sinews, and blood are what make up the

---

[77] For one Catholic artist's vision for the rebuilding of the tradition of sacred art, see David Clayton's reflections in "The Way
of Beauty," in *Second Spring: An International Journal of Faith
and Culture* 4 (2003): 19–26; see also Philip Bess, *Till We Have
Built Jerusalem: Architecture, Urbanism, and the Sacred* (Wilmington, Del: ISI Books, 2006).

real person. But he is misled. For, "to see 'the skull beneath the skin'" is to see the body and not the embodied person."[78] To have eyes only for the skull would be to miss the face. To see through everything leaves you, in fact, looking at nothing.

Overwhelmed by the power of science, we have too often allowed scientists to explain away the world they were trained to interpret. What is more, when knowledge is reduced to the empirical method, we not only lose the world of appearances; we can no longer even explain ourselves. Having abandoned the doctrine of creation—and with it any notion of final causality—we find that not only is the world left as an enigma, but the subject behind the research disappears. The materialist must see men and women as ghosts that haunt the very complicated machine that is the world. Here is what follows. In a disenchanted cosmos, the inner world is cut off from the outer. Romance, intuition, and art become separated from reason. So we leave it up to the artist to express our experience, while the scientist is supposed to explain laws that govern matter. The trouble is they never meet. In our contemporary schizophrenia, reason is indeed granted mastery over nature; but at a cost. Science has to admit the incomprehensibility of the mind, and the mind, for its part, gives up the right to travel outside of its own head. The net result is that science is reductive and our art irrational. No doubt, there are still fine novels and films. Mozart and J. S. Bach still live in concert halls; the arts and crafts movement carries on; and, particularly in North America, there are academies and architectural firms seeking to restore Neo-Classical and Neo-Gothic styles to the mainstream of our vernacular. But these are bottles in the sea. The dominant

[78] Put nicely by Roger Scruton in *Beauty* (Oxford: Oxford University Press, 2009), 70.

currents supported by both big business and the universities flow downstream. From text messages to rap to advertisement billboards to church art, everywhere we witness the exaltation of the vulgar, the rule of the irrational, and the triumph of bad taste.[79] Since Christian artists now generally follow secular culture as its late imitators, ecclesiastical arts suffer as secular arts.[80]

Debates over artistic questions in liturgy are nothing new. What is new is that we now doubt whether disagreements can be resolved by principles. Thus, when it comes time to build a new church, on questions of design, you typically find one of two patterns of discussion: either total war or total indifference. Usually there is no war. Where there are skirmishes, they are over money. Hardwood or carpet? Two bathrooms or three? An old-fashioned air-conditioner or an eco-friendly model? Such decisions surely require deliberation but not of the first order. After all, interesting debate assumes you hold some things in

---

[79] On this see studies by Robert Pattison, *The Triumph of Vulgarity: Rock Music in the Mirror of Romanticism* (Oxford: Oxford University Press, 1987) and by Thomas Day, *Where Have You Gone, Michelangelo: The Loss of Soul in Catholic Culture* (New York: Crossroads, 1993).

[80] Our churches have not fared well, but besides poor Latin translations, the introduction of imitation rock-and-roll music into our liturgies is likely the most damaging of all. The Church has consistently recommended Gregorian chant as the model for all liturgical music. As Pope Pius X concluded his lengthy discussion on church music: "On these grounds Gregorian Chant has always been regarded as the supreme model for sacred music, so that it is fully legitimate to lay down the following rule: the more closely a composition for church approaches in its movement, inspiration and savor the Gregorian form, the more sacred and liturgical it becomes; and the more out of harmony it is with that supreme model, the less worthy it is of the temple" (Pius X, *Motu Proprio* on sacred music, 3 [1903]).

common. We no longer can hold artistic principles in common, except by accident. Think of it this way: if beauty truly is only a matter of taste, then there is not much point in arguing about differences, since there would be, as a matter of fact, no method for resolving them, except by force.

Several steps in our intellectual history have led to our present confusion. Most decisively, the modern habit of isolating reason from artistic judgment goes back to Immanuel Kant.[81] His conclusion was that human reason could have knowledge only of material relations. As a consequence, God, morality, and beauty were rendered ultimately unknowable. I do not claim that Kant led directly to the Beatles. Nonetheless, the effects of Kant's theory of aesthetics were clear. Reason could no longer arbitrate,[82] and it left us standing with no arguments left to convince Mick Jagger to put his pants back on and no way to convince Janet Jackson that she ought to cover up. The point for us is this: modern art is almost uniformly a product of modern philosophy. The loss of beauty, form, and transcendence in John Cage, Van Gogh, and Le Corbusier is the result of the turn away from reason in Kant, Freud, and Nietzsche.

[81] As one of Kant's abler commentators has noted: "Kant's division of the mental faculties, into theoretical, practical and aesthetic (or, as he put it, understanding, practical reason and judgment), provided the starting point for all later investigations, and gave to aesthetics the central position in philosophy which it occupied through much of the nineteenth century and would, but for established scholasticism, occupy even now" in Roger Scruton, *The Aesthetics of Architecture* (Princeton, New Jersey: Princeton University Press, 1979), 1.

[82] One of the most incisive meditations upon this problem is George Grant's essay "Faith and the Multiversity," in *Technology and Justice* (Concord, Ontario: House of Anansi Press, 1986), 35–70.

Any return to older artistic sensibilities will require that we learn how to make the case once again that good style is also a matter of good sense.

But we are getting ahead of ourselves. The turn from premodern to modern forms of art obviously came about through intermediaries. We look at the connection between philosophy and modern liturgy as it affected only church architecture.

The rupture of the Church's architectural tradition is particularly grievous in light of its preeminence among the visual arts. Architecture is superior to painting and sculpture inasmuch as it defines not only two dimensions in surfaces (as in painting) nor exclusively three dimensions in volume (as in sculpture), but combines these along with a floor plan. This means, as the distinguished architectural historian Nikolaus Pevsner once pointed out, that "the good architect requires the sculptor's and the painter's modes of vision in addition to his own spatial imagination."[83] The architect thus defines space. In so doing he quite literally circumscribes the limits within which human culture moves. This power over space becomes the more critical when applied to ecclesiastical architecture. As the *Catechism* has it, church buildings "are not simply gathering places," but they make visible "the dwelling of God with men reconciled and united with Christ" (CCC 1180). The design of a church, in other words, is meant to offer a glimpse into what it is like to live with God. Churches symbolically prefigure the worship of Heaven. This is one reason the notion of a church being primarily built for "the gathered community" is silly. The community that gathers at a Mass is never simply the twenty or two hundred

[83] See Nikolaus Pevsner's illuminating comments in his introduction to *An Outline of European Architecture*, 5th ed. (London: Penguin, 1958), 23.

bodies occupying the pews. The gathered community at each Mass includes the whole Church, the *totus Christus*, the suffering, triumphant, and militant faithful united with Christ in Purgatory, in Heaven, and here on earth (CCC 954). Thus the stone and glass of a church is to produce an icon of this reality, "a symbol of the Father's house" (CCC 1186). As the founder of the University of Notre Dame's school of classical architecture, Duncan Stroik, memorably put it, churches are always a catechesis in stone.[84] A church is a *Catechism* that everyone can read. One that is badly built does more harm than one hundred sloppy books of theology.

All the parts of the building, like a living organism, serve a mystagogical function. As Abbot Suger, the great builder of the Abbey of St. Denis, the first Gothic church in Europe, wrote, the parts are to "urge us onward from the material to the immaterial" (*de materialibus ad immaterialia excitans*).[85] How does this work practically? Well, understanding even a single church can take years.[86] For us, it will be sufficient to consider its rudimentary elements.[87]

---

[84] A term used in his editorial in *Sacred Architecture* 14 (November 2008).

[85] Abbot Suger, *Liber de Rebus in Administratione* (34.33), in *On the Abbey Church of St.-Denis and Its Art Treasures*, ed., trans., and annotated by Erwin Panofsky, 2nd ed. (Princeton, New Jersey: Princeton University Press, 1979), 74.

[86] It took Margaret Visser, the Canadian classicist and writer on everyday rituals, several years to complete her study of the Romanesque parish church St. Agnes Outside the Walls in Rome; see her *The Geometry of Love: Space, Time, Mystery and Meaning in an Ordinary Church* (Toronto: HarperFlamingo, 2000).

[87] On the significance of the various elements of church design, paragraphs 1145–1186 of the *Catechism* are key; for general

On Sacraments

Our first step draws us into the narthex. This is the space immediately beyond the portal and signifies the transition between the world and the kingdom of God. Such a transition is necessary because of sin. We need to be shocked out of our complacency. Stepping into a church, in other words, should not be like walking into a shopping mall; it should be more like walking into Eden. So stepping into a church is a judgment against the world. Yet God loves the world, and so the church too is open to the world. All may enter—even the doubtful. It may take a curious onlooker several peeks into the narthex before he gathers the courage and the humility needed to get past the front door. Allowing space for these initial contacts is crucial.[88] Venture past the doors, and we enter a vast cosmos. The baptismal font marks our initiation into the life of grace: here Original Sin is scrubbed away. The holy water font reminds us of this first act of Christian initiation. We step next into the nave, from the Latin *navis*, or "ship." *Navis* evokes the tradi-

---

reference see *The Oxford Companion to Christian Art and Architecture*, by Peter and Laura Murray (Oxford: Oxford University Press, 1996); see also Steven J. Schloeder, *Architecture in Communion: Implementing the Second Vatican Council through Liturgy and Architecture* (San Francisco: Ignatius Press, 1998) and Denis R. McNamara, *Catholic Church Architecture and the Spirit of the Liturgy* (Chicago: Hillenbrand Books, 2009).

[88] This may be one reason to consider suppressing the habit of policing the narthex with professional greeters. Having sentinels on guard might make some feel welcome, but it is sure to turn others away. Requiring that everyone shake a hand presumptuously demands a level of comfort and familiarity that not all wish to offer. The narthex is a place of welcome in itself (more obviously so in large or cathedral churches) in that it allows the curious, the cautious, and the convicted a first means of approach.

tional understanding of the Church as the ark of salvation in the world. The nave thus represents our journey through time. Here is the place of our preparation for union with God made kneeling in confession (in the *Kyrie*), standing in praise (at the *Gloria*), and sitting in contemplative attention (during the *lectio*). All of this is offered by way of preparation for Communion. In the movement of the Mass we are going somewhere; we are heading to meet with God in the sanctuary, at the altar. The sanctuary is the fulfillment of the Jewish Holy of Holies. It is here at the altar that we gain entry to divine life through the eucharistic Communion. As the Eastern Orthodox theologian Alexander Schmemann has written on the transition between Jewish and Christian sacrificial worship:

> In "this world" there is no altar and the temple has been destroyed. For the only altar is Christ Himself, His humanity which He has assumed and deified and made the temple of God, the altar of His presence. And Christ ascended into heaven. The altar thus is the sign that in Christ we have been given access to heaven, that the Church is the "passage" to heaven, the entrance into the heavenly sanctuary, and only by "entering," by ascending to heaven does the Church fulfill herself, become what she is.[89]

In terms of design, the iconostasis in Eastern churches and the altar rail and raised sanctuary in the West mark this transition. Organically connected to Communion is, of course, adoration. It is an ancient teaching that eucharistic worship is

---

[89] A. Schmemann, *For the Life of the World* (Crestwood, New York: St. Vladimir's Seminary Press, 1973), 31.

incomplete without this loving contemplation. As St. Augustine provocatively wrote: *Nemo autem illam carnem manducat, nisi prius adoraverit; peccemus non adorando* — "No one eats that flesh without first adoring it; we should sin were we not to adore it" (*Ennarations on the Psalms* 98, 9; cited in SR 66). Obviously, all the prayers said in the Mass are to the Holy Trinity. But in the present dispensation, what Christians await is not the Comforter (whom the disciples awaited prior to Pentecost), but the return of the Redeemer. Christ will come again, and as the sun rises in the East so will the Sun of Righteousness return from the "East." This is one reason both the priest and the people have traditionally faced the east during its celebration, to anticipate the second coming of Christ.[90]

Settled in the belly of the nave, where do we look? Above all, the tabernacle serves to orient our prayer. The term comes from the word for "tent" and was prefigured in the Old Testament by the Ark of the Covenant. Historically this is where God's presence dwelt among the people in the desert. For Christians it likewise provides a house for God, now manifest bodily in the Eucharist. Its placement, accordingly, is vital. As the *Catechism* notes, it is to be situated "in a most worthy place and with the greatest honor" (CCC 1183). The tabernacle's displacement to the back corners and hidden recesses of some churches is perhaps the most poignant visual sign of the collapse of Catholic sensibility in recent decades.

Church design through the second half of the twentieth century largely abandoned its own symbolic language. As could have been predicted, reckless innovation in ritual led to the disorientation of the faithful. Instead of drawing from the

---

[90] On this see Ratzinger, *The Spirit of the Liturgy*, 74–84.

treasury of Christian symbolism, instead of acting as servants of a tradition, designers wanted to invent their own. Architects followed the lead of the German Bauhaus School and the French Le Corbusier (1887–1965), from which was adopted the principle that form follows function. What the leading schools of architecture failed to remember, however, is that one of the functions of a building is, precisely, to be *beautiful*. Modernist architecture was and remains self-consciously antitraditional. Following Kant, architects of this school not only separated the useful from the beautiful but, now moving beyond Kant, elevated function above beauty. Le Corbusier, for one, was fond of producing slogans. His 1923 *Vers Une Architecture* (translated as "Toward a New Architecture") captured the spirit of their iconoclastic movement in words such as:

A new epoch has begun.

There exists a new spirit.

There exists a mass of work conceived in the new spirit; it is to be met with particularly in industrial production.

Architecture is stifled by custom.[91]

In the modern era, the architect reveals himself as an artist, a creator; there is therefore "no longer any question of custom, nor of tradition ..." Thus "all values have been revised." Four thousand years of architectural styles are "no longer of any interest."[92] Putting flesh on these ideas, one of his more notable professional ambitions was to raze Paris to the ground and

[91] From *Towards a New Architecture*, trans. F. Etchells (New York: Frederick A. Praeger, 1965), 8.

[92] Ibid., 11–12, 268.

replace it with twenty-four identical multistory tower blocks.[93] Paris may have been saved, but few North American cities were spared; nor were our churches, for that matter. Those who concern themselves with the artistic idioms suitable for ecclesiastical art sometimes fail to grasp the connection between modern philosophy and modern art. In modernist architecture it is scientific rationalism plus democratic socialism that is translated into glass and steel.[94]

The break in the link between reason, nature, and beauty that assaulted twentieth-century philosophy did not *require* that our buildings and our liturgies become stripped of transcendence. For most of the Church's history, tradition ensured a substantial continuity of practice and belief even through disruptions in the realm of ideas. What has been most disastrous for the fine arts in the twentieth century, and in politics and morality for that matter, is the close tie between modern philosophy and society. When in 1793 leaders of the French Revolution plundered Notre Dame Cathedral in Paris, tearing down images of the Virgin Mary and replacing these with Lady Liberty, the iconography was prophetic. Abstract freedom, of course, can be used for a variety of purposes. But without a mooring in the natural law, in revelation, even in simple custom, the interpretation of freedom itself becomes highly contested. Societies born after the revolution became enslaved to

---

[93] See Ian Sutton, *Western Architecture: A Survey from Ancient Greece to the Present* (London: Thames and Hudson, 1999), 328.

[94] The revival of traditional architecture is by no means confined to theologians. Both the Congress for the New Urbanism and the International Network for Traditional Building, Architecture and Urbanism (INTBAU), for instance, are organizations—each with several thousand members—dedicated to promoting traditional design.

the vicissitudes of philosophers' opinions. Unfortunately, for the practice of liturgy, at the same moment that skepticism in ethics and art proved irresistible, so also was the idea of tradition made to look foolish, even in the Church. To make the point, we might imaginatively compare the overnight construction of a contemporary cathedral with the long development of, let us say, a typical English parish church. Built first in the twelfth century by the Normans, our parish church's Roman arches are replaced by Gothic ones in the thirteenth century; they are adorned with elaborate tracery in the perpendicular style in the fifteenth century. The glass is then smashed in the sixteenth, neglected in the eighteenth, restored by the Victorians in the nineteenth, and finally, along with the rest of the building, bulldozed in the twenty-first century to make room for a structure that reminds us more of Heathrow Airport than of Westminster Cathedral.

In theological terms, the turn in modern building meant that both the sacrificial nature of the Mass and the hierarchical structure of the priesthood were set aside in favor of an emphasis on community. Around the time of the council, the notion of active participation became transformed to mean not a deeper spirit of prayer but more pronounced *activity*. This turn in the Liturgical Movement had repercussions also for church architecture. Some of the more influential books written during the 1960s and 1970s had titles such as The Secular Use of Church Buildings and Everyday God: Encountering the Holy in World and Worship.[95] The focus had turned from Heaven to earth. Most church architects, following the steps of the leading modernist

[95] Both of these by J. G. Davis: *The Secular Use of Church Buildings* (New York: Seabury Press, 1968) and *Everyday God* (London: SCM Press, 1973).

architects, wanted buildings that were indeed functional. But that sentence is a fragment. To be intelligible you must specify *to what end* you wish your building to serve. Conviviality? Communication? Contemplation? All of the above? Worthy as these aims are, a church is first a temple of God. By contrast, for leading designers of the twentieth century, functionality meant emphasizing the immanence of the divine and the this-worldly purposes of religion.

Among the several important modernist theorists, I mention Peter Hammond. An Anglican priest, Hammond published the book *Liturgy and Architecture* (1960), which sought to upset the reign of Neo-Gothic, particularly in England. At one point in his book he defines the purpose of a church building in relation to this newer understanding of active participation:

> A church has no meaning apart from the community it serves. It is first and foremost a building in which the people of God meet to *do* certain things: to perform the various communal activities known collectively as liturgy, or public service. This is what the church is for.[96]

Notable among his recommendations was that the lectern should be dropped, leaving only a pulpit (this to emphasize the unity between the Scripture and preaching, presumably in order to stress the importance of offering relevant exegesis); he wanted less visual separation between sanctuary and nave (this was to lessen the gap between priest and people); the altar was to be free standing (so that the community could gather around

[96] *Liturgy and Architecture* (London: Barrie and Rockliff, 1960), 28, cited in Mark A. Torgerson, *An Architecture of Immanence: Architecture for Worship and Ministry Today* (Grand Rapids, Michigan: Eerdmans, 2007), 72.

it, in the manner of a meal); and, in general, distinctive archi-tectural details (one thinks here of statues of saints) were to be suppressed in favor of a more ecumenical style. The new church was to be a place of welcome for all Christians, not only Cath-olics. Through the *New Church Research Group*, which Ham-mond founded, a body comprising Catholics and Protestants, his ideas were influential in shaping the design of churches after Vatican II and outside of England as well.[97] Today few of these notions in church design sound revolutionary. But they once were.[98]

Conclusion

If cult is again to shape culture, Catholic worship must once more be rendered enchanting. Catholic architecture, like sacred music, sacred sculpture, and iconography, has a rich and varied language. The symbols and forms of Christian worship have developed organically alongside the liturgy as a means of enhancing the Church's central act of worship, the sacrifice of the Mass. In Aidan Nichols' terms, if the liturgy is once again to become enchanted and thus *enchanting*, a precondition is "the

---

[97] I follow here Torgerson's summary of Hammond's work in *An Architecture of Immanence*, 71–74; incisive criticism of Ham-mond is found in Schloeder, *Architecture in Communion*, 26.

[98] As when, for instance, Rembert G. Weakland, OSB (the future Archbishop of Milwaukee), wrote in 1980 against the value of tradition: "The further Church art, architecture, and music are removed from the contemporary idioms and styles of our times, the more likely it is that they will be sterile and artificial," in his essay "The Art and the Church," in *The Environment for Worship: A Reader*, ed. Secretariat, The Bishops' Committee on the Liturgy, National Council of Catholic Bishops (Washing-ton, DC: United States Catholic Conference, 1980), 9.

Our Lady of Guadalupe Shrine, LaCrosse, Wisconsin

eschewing of other uses to which—abusively—divine worship can be put."[99] In other words, liturgy must seek first to show the glory of the Lord; only afterward do we worry whether anyone is looking. In seeking to overcome the flight of beauty from our midst here are two theoretical and one practical conclusion we might draw. First, in philosophy, if we are to recover beauty in our art, we will need to learn how to heal the breach between reason and imagination that was introduced by metaphysical skepticism. Second, in liturgical theology: even to be useful for communities, churches must communicate transcendence. Finally, good ecclesiastical art comes at a high cost: for craftsmen, this cost is the long apprenticeship that is required of those who would serve within a tradition of inherited skills and symbols; for the rest of us, it is a price we would be impoverished to refuse to pay.

[99] Nichols, *Christendom Awake*, 21.

Rebuilding Catholic Culture

Is there reason for hope? Surely. The longed-for revival of traditional church architecture is now well underway. One might point, for instance, to the newly dedicated *Our Lady of the Most Holy Trinity Chapel* at Thomas Aquinas College, California, or to the Marian Shrine of *Our Lady of Guadalupe* in Wisconsin; on the East Coast, the Diocese of Raleigh's *Holy Name of Jesus Cathedral* will be the first classically inspired cathedral built in North America since Vatican II. A modest recovery of the Church's architectural tradition will take an entire generation, at least. Still, if the numerous churches recently built or renovated according to traditional designs are any indication of what can be achieved by the faithful, the work will well reward.

St. Thomas Aquinas, Italian,
c. 1450, hand-colored woodcut

5

On Virtue:
How Character Forms Conscience

Virtue and the happy life

In the midst of his travels throughout Palestine, Jesus encountered every type of human. Desperate outlaws, ambitious mothers, a noble centurion—the whole stream of humanity seemed to flow past our Lord as he walked along those dusty roads and weaved through those forgotten villages.

There is one figure, however, who appears most enigmatic. I refer to the young aristocrat. The youth is a puzzle because more than any other figure in the Gospels he lifts to us a mirror that reveals an image both familiar and foreign. You remember what he asked: "Teacher, what good must I do to have eternal life?" (Matt. 19:16). With this question he articulates, as often only the young can, that most basic of all human questions: What *good* must I do? This question is unavoidable. You cannot *not* act; to choose anything is to move toward some end. Which ones?

The young man asks and asks well. Even more, he is alive to his own best interest. "What good must I do" is followed by, "so that I might have eternal life." There is no one who does not seek his own happiness; and that happiness, to be complete, must be perpetual, secure from loss, eternal. Even in this life no one hopes to fall in love only for the summer.

We should not think of the rich young man as rapacious. He has wealth, to be sure, but also education and obligations. From what we can infer, the youth was well bred and well endowed. He is conscientious; he is the son of observant Jews, "raised in the shadow of the Law of the Lord" (VS 8). He knows the Torah and is able to answer the rabbi intelligently. He recognizes that there is a hierarchy within justice; so when Jesus replies that he must keep the law, the young man is bold to press his case. Which laws? Jesus replies: "You shall not commit adultery. You shall not steal ... Honor your father and your mother...." The twenty-something-year-old retorts with steady gaze: "I have kept all these." A bold answer, certainly, and Jesus' response bears no trace of incredulity. He accepts the young man's virtue, so far as it has been examined, then adds one last instruction: Become perfect! The command is cast in the form of a conditional. *If* you wish to become perfect, sell all you have, *and* follow me, *then* you will have treasure in Heaven (Matt. 19:21). The young man rejects Jesus' offer: "But when the young man heard these words he went away sad, for he was a man of great wealth." He goes away sad. He is forgotten like some skipping stone that slips beneath the surface of the water.

If we focus on the face of this young man that appeared so intently before our Lord, we see our own image. We recognize this same yearning for happiness, this same quest to know the meaning of our freedom. Many times finding out the correct question to ask can be the most difficult part of a problem. Well, the rich young man's problem is our problem; in his encounter with Christ, he helps us to see likewise what it is that we should ask of our Lord. The first question in ethics, then, is not "What am I obliged to do?" Nor is it "What is permitted?" The first question is "How can I be *happy?*" This is what Jesus answers for the rich young man; this is also what Christ reveals through his Sermon on the Mount in the Beatitudes. As with his word to the young man, to every man, Christ takes up the Old Testament promises to the Chosen people and reveals how we can become truly *beatus*, blessed, happy. Rooted in Scripture, nourished by the Fathers and great scholastics, the Church's moral teaching is first of all an answer to our quest for happiness. In its desire to renew the Church's traditional teaching, the Second Vatican Council called for a return to the original and primary sources of the faith. In the renewal of moral theology, in particular, this means a return to the question of *happiness.*[100]

From the rich young man we learn not only with what question we should begin; we see also how truth can be ignored. Having been told what will make him happy, the young man, mysteriously, turns back. This is not a case where the student left class unconvinced. Rather, he went away sad *because* he had great wealth. For our part, we should not be distracted by his money. The young man's attachment could have been to anything—sex, reputation, travel, his iPod. The enigma is that seeing the good, he rejects it. So do we. Why do we? In the young man's quest and then refusal of his own good we see with terrifying clarity our own condition: desiring happiness, we can still will our own demise. Faith is necessary because we have become nature's monster. "I do not understand what

---

[100] The leading Catholic moral theologian of recent times, Fr. Servais Pinckaers, OP, offers a compelling account of what such a renewed theology might look like in his *Morality: The Catholic View*, trans. M. Sherwin, OP (South Bend, Indiana: St. Augustine's Press, 2003).

I do," wrote St. Paul in his letter to the Romans; "I do not act as I mean to, but I do the things I hate" (Rom. 7:15). Unlike other creatures our nature is divided against itself. Being rational, we seek ends that reason perceives as good; being fallen, we will what is contrary to our will. John Donne (1572–1631) described this experience:

> I, like an usurpt town, to another due,
> Labor to admit you, but oh, to no end,
> Reason your viceroy in me, me should defend,
> But is captived, and proves weak or untrue.
>
> (Sonnet 14, *Holy Sonnets*)

As another poet has written, we are, "time's eunuch, and not breed one work that wakes."[101] Plunged into this raging sea of time and of our passions, man finds himself both the victim and perpetrator of the *mysterium iniquitatis*, the mystery of evil. And all the religions of the world, all the aching poetry, all the delicate philosophy of ages past and present attest to this universal desire for deliverance (CCC 28). Over the racket of the world and its distractions, the rich young man's question remains: "What good must I do to attain eternal life?" It is into this storm that God becomes man. And faith is the clutch of a drowning man's hand around the neck of his rescuer (CCC 26).

* * *

In our stroll through the *Catechism* we have now reached the halfway point. What is left to explore? "What faith confesses, the sacraments communicate": that was the theme of parts 1

---

[101] From G.M. Hopkins' poem "Justus quidem tu es, Domine," written in the last year of his life (1889), in *Gerard Manley Hopkins*, ed. C. Phillips (Oxford: Oxford University Press, 1990), 183.

On Virtue

and 2 (CCC 1692). Parts 3 and 4 turn to our response, in the moral life and through prayer. We might think of the structure this way. While the first half of the *Catechism* describes the *exitus* of God's self-revelation, the second outlines the *reditus* of the Christian's journey: procession and return forming the pattern of the Christian mystery. In the Creed and through the sacraments the Blessed Trinity communicates to us the goal of salvation and the supernatural means congruent with it. Prayer and the virtues constitute our response. Of course, nothing succeeds without grace, and recognizing our responsibility to move toward God does not lead us a step closer to Pelagius.

We are moved to care for our sick parents, to raise families, to build churches, not first because of duty, but because of *joy*. Sheer delight and excess of gratitude are the first impulses from which we act. There are duties in the Christian life, but joy comes first. As Benedict XVI emphasized in his encyclical *Deus Caritas Est*, charity is the fruit of our experience of being loved by the God who is love (DC 1). Love is born of God. Nevertheless what comes into focus in the second half of the *Catechism* is the need for our *cooperation*. As the Church's first *Catechism*, the second-century *Didache*, puts it: "There are two ways, the one of life, the other of death" (*Didache*, 1.1; quoted in CCC 1696). Both roads lie open before us; we must will to unite ourselves with God's work. The gospel is a message of glad tidings. It is also a rope thrown to a drowning man.

Section 1 of the *Catechism*'s third part addresses virtue and the moral conscience; section 2 looks at the Ten Commandments. The nature and function of conscience is arguably that aspect of moral theology most widely misunderstood. Terms such as *sin, guilt,* and *atonement* have all but lost their currency in the busy marketplace of public speech, but not conscience.

Agnostics become sentimental, and religious people whisper in hushed tones once conscience is slipped onto the table. When someone draws the card in debate, they do so often as though this were the one wild jack that everyone should recognize as trump. Of course, that is nonsense. I hope to make clear in what sense it is nonsense.

In this introduction to the *Catechism*'s moral theology we will look first to the relation between the virtues and our conscience, and after that to some obstacles that stand in the way of the kind of renewal which the Second Vatican Council called for.

Virtues and our conscience

At a high point—perhaps the height—of the Second Vatican Council's rhetoric on freedom, *Gaudium et Spes* defined conscience as "man's secret core and sanctuary," the place where "he is alone with God" (GS 16; CCC 1776). Such language has been misinterpreted.

To offer a benign example of how traditional concepts can be taken out of context, I point to Robert Bolt's popular 1960 drama of the life of St. Thomas More, *A Man for All Seasons*. As a meditation upon the courage of one man who stood against a despot, there is much to commend in the play. And yet, in the script, More ends up looking a little too much like a member of the American Civil Liberties Union and his martyrdom a protest against King Henry's breach of the First Amendment clause. Incidentally, some of Bolt's key lines come close to the language of the council, as when More tells his friend Norfolk (now an interrogator) why he cannot agree to the king's marriage, as Norfolk did:

On Virtue

St. Thomas More, Felix Bracquemond
after Hans Holbein the Younger

And when we stand before God, and you are sent to Paradise for doing according to your conscience, and I am damned for not doing according to mine, will you come with me, for fellowship? (Act 2, scene 6)

To which Thomas Cranmer replies: "So those of us whose names are there are damned, Sir Thomas?" And More: "I don't know, Your Grace. I have no window to look into another man's conscience. I condemn no one." It is fitting that Bolt should have More speak this way, since as he explains in his preface, as an agnostic Bolt aimed to depict More as a "hero of selfhood." Inspired by the existentialist writer Albert Camus, Bolt hoped to craft a stable point of reference for the self "without resort to magic." Bolt—and we can take him to stand in for all those interested in secular therapies—wants to find an immortal soul even after God is dead.[102] To treat conscience as man's secret and untouchable core fit well with the received wisdom of the 1960s. In popular psychology it was captured in the phrase, "I'm okay, you're okay." Or, as a university professor of mine used to quip ironically: "You're okay; how about me?" Of course, finding oneself alone with God in your conscience, unlike the impression Bolt's More leaves, is not a safe place to be. Refuge in this sanctuary purchases no automatic immunity (GS 16; CCC 1791).[103]

Bolt's play gives some insight into the spirit of the 1960s. But that spirit has animated not only playwrights; even some bishops have attempted to treat conscience as an infallible guide. Earlier I mentioned the "Winnipeg Statement" of the Canadian Bishop's Conference. Despite the objectively disordered nature of contraceptive acts, the document purported to explain how couples using artificial contraception might "in good conscience" regard themselves as in good standing within the Church. A more recent cause célèbre erupted over a statement issued by Walter Kasper and two other high-profile

---

[102] Robert Bolt, *A Man for All Seasons* (Toronto: Bellhaven House, 1974), xiii–xiv.

[103] Catholic Tradition has long distinguished between culpable and non-culpable errors of judgment (cf. CCC 1790–1802). As John Paul II writes: "Paul's admonition urges us to be watchful, warning us that in the judgments of our conscience the possibility of error is always present. Conscience *is not an infallible judge*; it can make mistakes. However, error of conscience can be the result of an *invincible ignorance*, an ignorance of which the subject is not aware and which he is unable to overcome by himself" (emphasis original) (VS 62).

German bishops. In a pastoral letter dated July 10, 1993, the bishops recommended that under certain circumstances, divorced and "remarried" individuals who engage in sexual acts might receive Communion. The statement was shortly overturned by the Vatican.[104] But the rationale of the bishops illustrates well the effects of unduly isolating and elevating conscience. In their letter the pastors made clear that they had no wish to abrogate the Church's teaching on the indissolubility of marriage. Nevertheless, they hoped to offer a new pastoral guideline. Instead of denying divorced and remarried Catholics Communion, they argued that a "remarried" individual could receive the Eucharist if, after "a personal review of his or her conscience," an individual were to determine that he or she should receive. The bishops concluded: "The priest will respect the judgment of the individual's conscience, which that person has reached after examining his own conscience and becoming convinced of his approaching the holy eucharist can be justified before God."[105]

What interests us is the view of conscience tacitly assumed within their argument. Those finding fault with the bishops' statement pointed out that, given the Church's teaching, under no conditions could such a determination of conscience,

[104] See "Letter to the Bishops of the Catholic Church Concerning Reception of Holy Communion by the Divorced and Remarried Members of the Faithful," issued by the Congregation for the Doctrine of the Faith, September 14, 1994.

[105] Citations from the bishops' letter taken from the translation provided by *Origins* 23, no. 38 (March 10, 1994): 674, 675. As the bishops further state: a priest should give particular weight to a "remarried" person's judgment "especially ... when the conscience is convinced that the earlier, irreparably destroyed marriage was never valid" (p. 674).

however sincere, be valid.[106] Since a valid marriage is indissoluble, the Catholic Church cannot recognize the legal possibility of divorce. Therefore, an individual who divorces and engages in conjugal relations with another commits adultery, which is always wrong. Such has been the Church's long-standing teaching (cf. CCC 1650; FC 84). As Cardinal Ratzinger pointed out in his response to the bishops, divorced persons who remarry civilly "find themselves in a situation that objectively contravenes God's law," and consequently, "they cannot receive Holy Communion as long as this situation persists" (LRC 4).

Even if in a person's heart of hearts he believes his previous marriage to be invalid, this does not guarantee that it is so. Marriage is not a private affair. The consent that binds two people establishes a social and ecclesial reality. Hence, the judgment of conscience "does not regard only the immediate relationship between man and God"; rather, that judgment "also includes canonical laws binding in conscience" (LRC 8). In other words, an informed conscience is not an isolated conscience. Conscience must judge based upon facts. One of the moral facts that must be taken into account is the teachings of the Church.

Clearly the German bishops were confused. Nowhere did they define what they meant by *conscience*; nor did they explain how it abrogated such authority to itself. Our question of the bishops is not so much what motivated them to test Church teaching. Rather, what is most intriguing is: What did they imagine conscience to be? Sadly, we can only infer that like many others the bishops had imagined conscience to be isolated,

---

[106] See the public letter of reply to the German bishops by Germain Grisez, John Finnis, and William May published in the *Fellowship of Catholic Scholars Newsletter* (June 1994): 20–27.

sovereign, and alone. Demanding conscience carry a weight it was never created to bear does not honor God's gift. Separating conscience from law, from the Church, and from custom cuts it off from its roots in reality. Conscience so conceived becomes a tyrant because, separated from objective norms, it no longer knows whom or what it should serve.

Maimed from birth, corrupted through custom, enslaved by habit, conscience is a guide that, untutored, will lead us astray. We are right to praise conscience. Its presence is one mark of our dignity as children of God. Even so, as John Henry Newman put it, "Conscience has rights because it has duties."[107] The *Catechism* relates: "The education of conscience is indispensible for human beings who are subjected to negative influences and tempted by sin to prefer their our judgment and to reject authoritative teachings" (CCC 1783). Conscience is a guide, but we are warned: the tide of human judgment runs downstream. For this reason the Church begs her Lord to "heal our troubled conscience."[108] Lazily floating along the river of life with a raft filled only with other fellows and good times will not eventually land you on a sandy beach but will carry you over a steep fall. The eighteenth-century novelist Oliver Goldsmith's quip comes to mind: "Conscience is a coward; and those faults it has not strength enough to prevent it seldom has justice

---

[107] See further VS 34 here citing Newman's "Letter to the Duke of Norfolk," §5.

[108] From *The Liturgy of the Hours*, week 2, Friday morning prayer after Psalm 51: "Father, he who knew no sin was made sin for us, to save us and restore us to your friendship. Look upon our contrite heart and afflicted spirit and heal our troubled conscience, so that in the joy and strength of the Holy Spirit we may proclaim your praise and glory before all the nations."

enough to accuse."[109] The question for us: How to strengthen the muscle? How to bend our consciences (and others') so that we do not fall over the edge? The answer in brief, is this: acquire virtue.

> The human virtues are stable dispositions of the intellect and will that *govern* our acts, *order* our passions, and *guide* our conduct in accordance with reason and faith. (CCC 1834)

Virtues are stable dispositions. They govern, order, and guide our conduct. In short: character forms conscience; character is the sum of your virtue; therefore, if you wish to become someone who consistently makes right judgments of conscience, train in virtue. To chart the route of that climb we shall, in the next chapter, take Dante as our guide, but before we step onto Mount Purgatory, I want to clear away some of the debris that lies in our way.

Relativism and the ethics of authenticity

There are two features of our contemporary thinking about moral action that make the recovery of the Christian notion of conscience all but impossible. Both of these "stones" have to be removed if we are to appropriate again the language and practice of the virtues. The first barrier on our path is the stone of historical distance, and the second, the stone of modern psychology.

First is the problem of historical distance. Between us and the Christian language of conscience is the stone wall of several hundred years of intervening moral philosophy. Our lack

---

[109] From his novel *The Vicar of Wakefield* (1762), ch. 13.

of education in the history of ideas is what erects this barrier. The language of conscience deployed in the *Catechism* is based upon a conceptual apparatus that found its high expression in the medieval scholasticism of eight hundred years ago. Needless to say, that imposing edifice has been largely abandoned. Appeal to conscience presupposes a highly developed tradition of moral reasoning in which the adjacent concepts of natural law, virtue, and sin, and also happiness, hold integral parts. For many of us, these concepts have been drained of their meaning. When we speak of what is noble in man today, we are not accustomed to draw from the language of Plato, Aristotle, or St. Thomas Aquinas, but of more recent thinkers. Drawing once again from these ancient sources would require, at the least, recognition of what has come in between.

Here is an analogy that illustrates the difficulty. Many of the great European and North American cathedrals still occupy their original geographical locations. But everything around them has changed. No longer is Cologne Cathedral the tallest building in the world (as it was for a time in the nineteenth century), and St. Patrick's is buried in the shadow of Manhattan's skyscrapers. Their surroundings have altered; and so have we. Most of our neighbors enter churches only as tourists. The symbols mostly have to be explained. The same now holds true with the old language of morality. Sometimes we mouth the words that others did, but their sounds have taken on a different sense. Often we do not even use the same words.

Take, for instance, the term *values*. In our language, *values* now substitutes for good and evil.[110] For one thing, there is no

[110] This and the next paragraph borrow from and extend a similar discussion of mine in R. Topping, *St. Augustine* (London: Continuum, 2010), 36–37.

obvious equivalent to *values* in either Greek or Latin. The near-est candidates in Latin are *bona* (goods), *mores* (habits, morals), and *vota* (prayers, vows). Furthermore, the idea of there being such a thing as moral values (in the plural) entered our lexicon only recently. I note that the Oxford English Dictionary lists as their earliest example of values (in the plural) a passage taken from a 1918 sociological text. *The Polish Peasant in America* ana-lyzes the emigration of Continental Europeans to the United States during the latter part of the nineteenth and early-twenti-eth centuries.[111] The nineteenth-century European emigration mirrors the transatlantic migration of ideas that was carried to the New World by the emerging disciplines of psychology and sociology, by Sigmund Freud (1856–1939), and by Max Weber (1864–1920).

Values entered our common usage not through the classical or Romance languages but through the German *Werte*, as in *sittliche Werte*, "moral values."[112] This shift from *value* to *values* (in the plural) was the product of German genius. Its clearest expression is found in Nietzsche's little work *Jenseits von Gut*

---

[111] The text is *The Polish Peasant in Europe and America*, 5 vols. (1918–1920) by Thomas and Znaniecki, from which the OED gives this excerpt: "Sociology ... has this in common with social psychology: that the values which it studies draw all their reality, all their power to influence human life, from the social attitudes which are expressed or supposedly expressed in them."

[112] Although English takes value from the French *valoir* (to be of worth) and the Latin *valere* (to be strong, powerful), its meta-morphosis into the plural values was the work of other influ-ences; the nearness in morphology between the singular and the plural should not blind us to their distance in semantics. The two words have about as much to do with each other as do *bread* and *bred*.

On Virtue

und Böse (*Beyond Good and Evil: Prelude to a Philosophy of the Future*), published in 1886. So, we might say that we live in Nietzsche's crystal ball. What did he see? Recall that Nietzsche was a cultural relativist. To him values are expressions of will. They are created, not discovered. Values are *beyond* good and evil in the sense that they stand prior to and are the source of the particular moralities that define "cultures." Values are the created horizons against which lesser men chart their courses. True creators are few. Among them Nietzsche named Moses, Jesus, and Mohammed. But by an act of supreme irony, once Nietzsche was transplanted into the soil of American egalitarianism, his teaching, like Proteus, assumed an altogether different form. Values in the English-speaking nations are no longer the currency in which only the rarest and most aristocratic of souls trade: to us they are not the products of supermen, but of everyman. Even high school students can create them, if they choose.

As regards sex, individual or group lifestyles are based upon values that you discovered when you were fifteen, and if you have a midlife crisis, you can revamp when you turn forty. Your sexual values will have been articulated for you in a high school sex-education or "Lifestyles" course. Having found the pearl of great price at the end of a high school dance, nothing of what you learn in college will tell you anything you didn't already know. You will become more sophisticated; you will become less inhibited; you will learn how to think for yourself. English, psychology, and sociology professors will even help you defend the conviction that nothing should come between you and another consenting adult.[113] Naturally, sex can even be

[113] The most accessible discussion of the bizarre fate of Nietzsche on the North American continent is found in Allan Bloom,

healthy recreation, like hockey and squash—so long as you wear the right protective equipment. On the political level, within liberal democracies the fusion of liberal egalitarianism with German relativism has produced a most surprising cocktail: multiculturalism. In Canada, for example, by some miracle of state-sponsored tolerance, "Canadian values," "Native values," "family values," certainly "gay" and possibly "Saudi" values are all welcome to find their home within the tapestry of Canadian's welcoming society.[114] Every soul finds a home in the true North without fear of contradiction—as long as you don't mind feeling a bit queasy inside. What applies there applies elsewhere. You're okay; am I okay?

When we do not speak the language of Nietzsche, two other modern traditions of moral discourse are available to us. These are the languages of *rights* and of *authenticity*, Locke's Liberalism and Rousseau's Romanticism. The first governs our public philosophy; the second governs our private lives. The morality of universal rights dictates the rules of the office; the rule of authenticity sets the pace for after hours. We have already spoken of some of the difficulties involved in adopting rights language apart from a doctrine of creation, so here we will offer just a few remarks on the language of authenticity.

What Rousseau tried to describe in his *Emile* was the education of the natural man. This is modernity's one and only attempt to produce an image of human excellence that can rival the heroes of the pagan and Christian worlds, the sage, the soldier, and the saint. Thus, to the ideal of the philosopher,

---

The Closing of the American Mind (New York: Basic Books, 1987), 194–226.

[114] For a recent study of features of the Canadian experience see Ezra Levant's *Shakedown*.

Jean-Jacques Rosseau, Pierre-Michel Alix

the knight, and Francis and Clare, we can add *Emile* — the first authentically modern human being. At the root of this tradition is the distinction between authentic and inauthentic self-regard. Rousseau's terms are *amour de soi* (healthy self-love) and *amour-propre* (vain regard). The first is love of self based upon nature; the second is other-oriented self-regard and, as Rousseau thinks, rooted only in convention. As he says,

> Self love (*amour de soi*), which regards only ourselves, is contented when our true needs are satisfied. But *amour propre*, which makes comparisons, is never content.[115]

In this view, unhappiness is caused when our judgments of value are based on the opinions of others. Dependent judgment

---

[115] Jean-Jacques Rousseau, *Emile*, trans. Allan Bloom (New York: Basic Books, 1979), bk. 4, 213–224.

is unnatural judgment: it delivers over to others the freedom and autonomy that belongs properly to ourselves. And there is truth to this. One element of the virtuous life must surely include a hearty contempt of following fashion simply because it is fashionable. Fidelity, constancy, and independence of mind are qualities that allow us to remain steady before adversity, to follow truth when it is not convenient, and to suffer persecution when necessary. After the slaughter of two World Wars, instigated as they were by totalitarian regimes, it was proper that the rights of conscience be asserted at the Second Vatican Council. But there are risks to such a line of defense. Freedom of conscience needs to be defended by reason; but conscience alone is a frail defense if what you really hope to secure is human dignity.

What Rousseau introduced into modern thought was the notion that the dividing line that runs through men's hearts cuts not between virtue and vice (the classical view), nor between sin and original justice (the distinctive Christian contribution), but between authenticity and insincerity, good faith and bad (the Romantic modern view). The real conflict, in short, is the struggle between being inner-directed and being outer-directed, between looking to oneself and looking to others for moral guidance.[116] Not the fall but "dependence on other men" is what "ruptures [the natural man's] original unity or wholeness."[117]

Before we even reach the foot of Mount Purgatory we must overcome this first obstacle. We are separated from the Christian view of conscience by the vast divide of history, the first

---

[116] In Kant's terminology, this became the difference between heteronomy and autonomy.

[117] See Allan Bloom's comments in his introduction to *Emile*, 4.

stone. Between ourselves and the scholastics—where the language of conscience definitively found a home—lies the modern and postmodern cult of authenticity.

Once the first barrier is mounted, the second is easy to spot. The second stone is the modern faith in earthly perfection. Christian morality assumes sin. The Good News is an answer to the bad news that all is not well. For Rousseau, by contrast, man is born whole. Natural education aims to keep him that way; it is only contact with others that corrupts.[118] Where Christians speak of sin Rousseau's heirs in the social sciences speak of maladjustment. Systems, not sinners, are the real trouble. In our sophistication we have ceased to blame envy and greed and instead direct our animus against "structures of oppression." According to the Creed of the Apostles, history is not primarily the overcoming of economic inequality; it is, rather, the unfolding of the divine comedy, the drama of man's liberation from cosmic and personal evil. Once the Christian doctrine of Original Sin is understood, Christian ambivalence toward conscience becomes inevitable. The *Catechism* explains why conscience, although honored, is nothing divine; it explains also why those who pray at its temple must also pay the price of settling for a self that, although free, lives alone, naked, and in splendid isolation.

Conclusion

From the above sketch it should be obvious that any simple transposition of "conscience" into the contemporary scene runs aground from the outset. To rehabilitate conscience would require both an understanding of the origins of the new

---

[118] Rousseau, *Emile*, 440.

language of morality and an immersion in the old one that we have forgotten. As the meanings of natural law, virtue, sin, and charity recede from our common understanding, the appeal to isolated concepts, such as *conscience* and *freedom*, plucked at random from the vast orchard of the Christian tradition, yields results more and more bizarre. Only good fruit can go bad. In the modern world, the good fruit cultivated over centuries within Christendom has gone very bad indeed. In recent years Catholic hospitals, adoption agencies, and schools have lost much of their institutional independence. Insofar as those entrusted with Catholic institutions continue to pursue a policy of deference and accommodation to secularism, the trend will continue. Already in 1987 Cardinal Ratzinger recognized the vacancy of such hopes. He ridiculed what he called the "guileless progressivism" of the early postconciliar years, which like "a model schoolboy" strove to prove the compatibility of the Faith with all things modern. Today we need a different strategy. The Church can truly serve the world only when she offers to it the message that has been given from above:

> A Christianity that believes it has no other function than to be completely in tune with the spirit of the times has nothing to say and no meaning to offer. It can abdicate without more ado. Those who live vigilantly in the world of today, who recognize its contradictions and its destructive tendencies ... such people do not look to Christianity for approbation but for the prophetic salt that burns, consumes, accuses, changes.[119]

---

[119] Joseph Ratzinger, *Principles of Catholic Theology: Building Stones for a Fundamental Theology*, trans. Sr. M. F. McCarthy (San Francisco: Ignatius Press, 1987), 56.

On Virtue

The falsely Romantic premises assumed by the *New York Times*, the *Globe and Mail*, and *The Guardian* need to be challenged. Tacitly concede cultural relativism or the ethics of authenticity, and the language of conscience becomes a weapon in enemy hands. If Christians wish to appeal to conscience in debate, they must be ready to articulate why the fact of Original Sin makes reason's education in tradition necessary. Otherwise, if Rousseau is right and children really are born whole, then there is no place for Hell and no need for Purgatory either. We may summarize the key statements that the *Catechism* makes about conscience this way: Conscience is a judgment of reason (CCC 1778); it can judge moral actions rightly or wrongly (CCC 1786); therefore, we are obliged to form it well (CCC 1784). Like all training, learning to exercise the judgment of conscience requires an apprenticeship, an education. In the next chapter we will learn how conscience can go to school.

The Four Cardinal Virtues: Justice,
Netherlandish, 16th century, wool warp

On Law:
What Love Commands

Nobody likes a moralist. It is good that Christians have moved
beyond moralism. Moralism is always a diluting of religion, a
simplification. It is the faith of Pelagius and Kant, not of St.
Augustine and Bishop Bossuet. Love for the good and love for
the beautiful belong together. To moralize is to separate these
two, reducing faith to sheer obedience. It is an ancient truism
that the virtuous person not only does the good, but delights in
doing it (CCC 1770). When philosophers and preachers in the
middle of the twentieth century proclaimed that we had moved
beyond moralism, it was not always clear where they hoped we
would land. Christians rightly point out that love is at the center of ethics. And to love someone is to do him good.

But how do we know what is good? Is it discovered through
conscience, intuition, law, or something else entirely? In what
follows I hope to show how Dante's *Divine Comedy* can serve as
an orientation to the study of such questions specifically and to
Catholic moral theology generally.

Law and Christian liberty

Unlike Dante's age, ours has grown accustomed to living
with fragmentary and even competing accounts of the good

Jacques-Bénigne Bossuet, Gerard Edelink,
Flemish, c. 1700, etching and engraving

life. Even among Christians it is difficult to find agreement as
to which principles are primary in our moral deliberations. In
popular teaching traditional categories such as a *law* or *duty*
are often derided. Recent years have seen something of a turn
in this trend, however. The problems with an exclusive reliance upon social-scientific (and hence "value free") accounts
of human action have become evident. Even if we do not know
how to integrate older categories within our moral reasoning,
it has become plain that liberating ourselves from notions such
as *moral law* can have terrifying consequences. One recent case
will illustrate.

In 2010, in the face of gross misconduct, the Irish government initiated two separate judicial reviews to determine the
extent and causes of corruption among the nation's Catholic
hierarchy. The Murphy Commission, in particular, investigated
the bishops' handling of allegations of sexual misconduct among

priests in the Diocese of Dublin from 1975 to 2004, which has led to the resignation of several auxiliary bishops of Dublin. Any breach of trust by clergy is occasion for scandal, sorrow, and restitution. But what has caused outrage in the case of Ireland and several other jurisdictions is the way that bishops failed to discipline clergy even after allegations were substantiated. Offending priests were often simply shuffled from one parish to another. In the case of the diocese of Dublin, Justice Murphy has pointed to how disregard for canon law among bishops and clergy sheltered repeat offenders and exposed the vulnerable. The report notes how, in Dublin, "the Church authorities failed to implement most of their own canon law rules on dealing with clerical child-sexual abuse." Not that Church law was inadequate. "The Commission is satisfied that Church law demanded severe penalties for clerics who abused children. In Dublin, from the 1970s onwards, this was ignored."

It is not the case, in other words, of the law's being under- or over-specified; laws were simply not heeded. Observing what has become shamefully plain, the report links the neglect of justice to the disrespect of law within the Church more generally: "Canon law, as an instrument of Church governance, declined hugely during Vatican II and in the decades after it."[120] In countering what may have been an excessive legalism within pre–Vatican II Roman Catholic piety, pastors and theologians from the 1960s onward swung wildly in the opposite direction. Some replaced moralism with vague appeals to love and therapeutic approaches to inner healing that disregard the fact of sin and the

---

[120] Citations from the Commission taken from "The Wolves Roamed Freely: Recent Judicial Commission Reports Contain Devastating Findings about Abuse and Cover Up in the Irish Church," in *Catholic World Report* (February 2010): 28–30.

requirements of justice. Therapy has a place; but not if it sepa-
rates our aspiration for happiness from our obligations to love.[121]

As the second-century Church father St. Irenaeus (d. 202)
wrote: "The words of the Decalogue remain likewise for us
Christians" (*Adv. Haeres.*, 4, 16, 4; CCC 2063). The Law of the
Gospel "'fulfills,' refines, surpasses, and leads the Old Law to
its perfection" (CCC 1967). Law is amplified, and law is developed: its meaning is expanded and extended. In its explication
of moral theology the *Catechism* explains how the evangelical
counsels (CCC 1973), the beatitudes (CCC 1717), and the
whole of Christ's Sermon on the Mount unearth for Christians
hidden meanings of the Law.

What I wish to focus on is not how the Gospel reveals the
deeper significance of the Law, but how Law expands from a
written to an unwritten code. We still need laws on paper. But
in the New Covenant, law becomes internalized. In fulfillment
of Ezekiel's prophecy (Ezek. 37:1–14), the New Law rests not on
stones but in the hearts of the faithful through the gift of the
Holy Spirit.

And thus to our question: When Christ told the young ruler
to keep the commandments, he added also that the young man
must become perfect (Matt. 19:21). What would that look like?

There are few better visual guides than *The Divine Com-
edy*.[122] With an eye also to the *Catechism*, we will turn first to the

---

[121] On this see the works of Servais Pinckaers, OP; for instance,
his *Morality: The Catholic View*.

[122] Of the author of *The Divine Comedy*, Dante Alighieri, T.S.
Eliot once remarked: "Dante and Shakespeare divide the
modern world between them; there is no third" in his *Dante*
(originally published within his *Selected Essays*) (London:
Faber and Faber, 1965), 46.

structure of *The Divine Comedy* as a whole and then look to the geography of Mount Purgatory. From the poem we can draw four lessons that illuminate the *Catechism's* moral vision: the pedagogical function of pleasure and pain; the nature of the act of conscience; the doctrine of the mean; and the primacy of love.

Pedagogy in The Divine Comedy

In *The Divine Comedy*, Purgatory is situated, naturally, between Hell and Heaven. Any of the poem's three parts would offer instruction on the moral life, although the second is suited especially to our purposes. In Hell there is no hope; Heaven contains no struggle; only Purgatory, like earth, remains a site for progress. Within this finest of all Christian poems the *Purgatorio* presents an allegory of our ascent through the virtues. *The Divine Comedy* is other things besides — political commentary, historical record, delicate verse — but first of all it is theology. Through the poem, Dante records the drama of the soul's choice either for or against its own good. Choose God, and the *Purgatorio* shows us what follows from that decision.

Dante's *Divine Comedy* is also an allegory, an extended metaphor. Its central images claim to be universal and thus contemporary. Put to use within prose or poetry, it is "the interpretation of experience by means of images."[123] Dante intends the structure and symbols of his poem to deliver an *argument*. No doubt there are certain decayed views of the value of art, transmitted to the English-speaking world chiefly through the young Oscar Wilde (1854–1900), which isolate art from reason and philosophy. The early twentieth-century movement of

---

[123] As Dorothy Sayers has said in her introduction to Dante's *Inferno* (London: Penguin, 1949), 11.

"art for art's sake" is an instance of this. Critics asserted that creative works retain their integrity if and only if they were sheltered from the conflicts and interests of politics, of religion, and even of daily life. Such aesthetes wanted to preserve art from the calculations of mere propaganda, which is correct, but they did so at the high cost of separating it from the demands of truth, which is banal. Anyway, since at least F.W.J. Schelling (e.g., his 1803 essay *Über Dante in philosophischer Beziehung*) the leading German, French (e.g., E. Gilson's *Dante et la philosophie*, 1939), and English (e.g., Dorothy Sayers' notes to *The Divine Comedy*, 1949–1962) interpreters have read Dante as also a

Allegorical Painting of Dante, Italian, late 16th century, oil on panel

philosopher.[124] And so shall we. As a poet, the use of images carries Dante's claims every bit as much as the use of mathematical signs carries to conclusion the proofs of a physicist. In the Catholic imagination, noble poetry (like noble architecture, painting, and music) fulfills its function best when it leads us by means of beauty, however subtly, to a greater love of the true and the good, lifting great art from the realm of the purely private.[125] This was also Dante's view of his work. So, for the reader with an interest in his own destiny, *The Inferno* acts as a solemn warning. Over the entrance to Hell is inscribed:

> *Nothing ere I was made was made to be*
> *Save things Eterne, and I eterne abide;*
> *Lay down all hope, you that go in by me.*
> (*Inf.*, cant. II, lines 7-9)

[124] To affirm that Dante's poem presents a philosophical argument in no ways suggests that either its interpretation or its assertions elicit universal agreement (criticism of Schelling's Romantic view of Dante can be seen, for instance, in Hans Urs Von Balthasar's *The Glory of the Lord, Vol. 5: The Realm of Metaphysics in the Modern Age* [San Francisco: Ignatius Press, 1991], 564); it is simply to contradict the position that poetry is incapable of stating universal claims. Orientation to Dante scholarship can be found in a set of entries "Dante in England," "Dante in France," "Dante in Germany," etc., in the *Dante Encyclopedia*, ed. Richard Lansing (New York: Garland Publishing, Inc., 2000), and in M. Caesar's *Dante: The Critical Heritage* (London: Routledge, 1999).

[125] On this see further John Paul II's *Letter to Artists*, in which he writes: "Insofar as [art] seeks the beautiful, as the fruit of an imagination which rises above the everyday, art is by its nature a kind of appeal to the mystery. Even when they explore the darkest depths of the soul or the most unsettling aspects of evil, artists give voice, in a way, to the universal desire for redemption" (10).

Passing through the gate Virgil remarks to his stricken companion,

> We've reached the place I told thee to expect,
> Where thou shouldst see the miserable race,
> Those who have lost the good of intellect.
>
> (Inf., cant. III, lines 16–18)

Having rejected the good, those in Hell find that reason is lost, and with it hope. Dante guides us through twenty-four circles of Hell, not to avenge his enemies, but to make clear the calamity of sin; by breathing in the stench of the Inferno, by watching the winds whip the lustful into the air (Inf., cant. V, line 31), by hearing the wail of suicides trapped within mangled bodies they sought to escape (cant. XIII, line 107), images add force to naked appeal. All our decisions count. With their effects before our senses we see with sharper vision the import of choices. God grants what we wish. The Inferno prods us to wish well.

By contrast, Paradiso instructs with caresses and sweet smells. Here we revel in the warm glow of Heaven and taste of the delight of the saints. Arriving at the fourth sphere of Heaven, the circle of teachers, Dante, and Beatrice meet St. Thomas Aquinas and eleven other souls. Brilliant in glory, bathed in light, the twelve sing music the poet cannot describe (Parad., cant. X, line 147).

And in the midst of this ringing joy Dante turns to us his readers with this encouragement:

> Bide on thy bench now, Reader, and think back
> Upon this foretaste, if the feast in store
> Thou wouldst enjoy ere relish tire and slack;

On Law

And if imagination cannot run
To heights like these, no wonder: no eye yet
E'er braved a brilliance that outshone the sun.
(*Parad.*, cant. X, lines 22–24, 46–48)

In the *Purgatorio*, we witness both kinds of appeal, and for good reason. Fundamentally there are only two passions within the human heart: repulsion and attraction (CCC 1763). In moral education, threats and punishments repel, while promises and rewards incline. Thus, in the *Comedy*, as in real life, the stench and screams of Hell are meant to instill fear of one possible end to earthly life, just as the songs and colors of Paradise inspire longing for another. That is the first lesson we should take away from Dante. Moral education begins with pleasure and pain. A purely cerebral approach to virtue ignores that we have bodies and treats us like talking heads. This is not to say that pleasure is the highest good, nor is it to reduce all pleasures to the body (the pleasure of study, for one, is an instance of a pleasure not linked to our senses [cf. Arist., NE 1153a]). It is to affirm, however, that until we are unaffected by passable experiences, until our will is resolutely settled, until our intellect is firmly fixed, we shall need to be trained by caresses and blows, constantly reaffirming the association between the good with the pleasant and the bad with the painful. Souls far advanced in spiritual progress report that eventually even material pleasure and pain will not count for us. Most of us never completely escape the rod in this life and are likely to start out with it in the next.

Purgatorio and the ascent of virtue

The right use of pleasure and pain is the first lesson that we learn by looking at the structure of the *Comedy*. The second, third, and fourth lessons we take from the geography of Purgatory itself. In Dante's vision, the mountain rises in the southern hemisphere of the earth, is surrounded by undisturbed waters, and is silent in its beauty. All is quiet except for occasional song and the shouts of *alleluias* heard each time a soul is freed to go to Heaven. (There is no singing in Hell.) Once Virgil and Dante alight upon the mountain, what do they see?

One of the virtues of the *Purgatorio* is that it provides a visual image, an icon, of the Catholic synthesis of classical and biblical sources. We see an instance of this in the motion of the stars. Alighting on the shore of Ante-Purgatory on Easter Sunday morning, Dante beholds four jewels glittering above. He records his first impression thus:

> Right-hand I turned, and, setting me to spy
> That alien pole, beheld four stars, the same
> The first men saw, and since, no living eye;
> (*Purg.*, cant. I, lines 1–3, 22–24)

In the poem we know that the four stars over Eden are, allegorically, the cardinal virtues. We know this because, unlike many other images, Dante declares their meaning to us directly in Canto 31. At the climax of the *Purgatorio*, at his meeting with Beatrice, four semi-divine maidens follow in her train as she prepares to lift Dante up to Paradise. They explain that although they appear now as nymphs, while he was on the mountain they looked to him as stars, ordained to lead him to Beatrice's eyes (*Purg.*, cant. XXXI, lines 106–111). Allegorically this expresses how Catholic moral theology presupposes the existence of natural virtue. Noble pagans are good pagans. But their goodness is incomplete. Natural virtue was given to man from the beginning of time to *prepare* him for the grace that would enter with the Incarnation. The cardinal virtues (i.e., prudence, fortitude, temperance, and justice) are necessary, but they are not sufficient. And besides, only Adam and Eve in their state of original justice saw these stars with perfect clarity. Since then we have perceived them truly, although through a darkened glass, through the spectacles of sin that we all wear.[126]

In Western intellectual history, Plato's *Republic* provides the first systematic outline of the cardinal virtues.[127] There Plato singled out three characteristically human activities: thinking, willing, and desiring. Except while asleep, every living person does these things, for the Greeks soul, or *psyche* (literally, breath), is that which animates life. Its presence marks the difference between your dog Lassie sitting at your feet and a cold corpse. All living things have a soul, and ours is rational.

According to Plato the three activities of the soul correspond to its three parts. The virtuous person is that one whose soul (and each of its parts) fulfills its proper functions. Now, to say that virtue is the perfection of the soul, as Plato and Aristotle did, is to say that the various functions of the soul are operating in a good order. It is in relation to these differentiated activities that we can learn something about the specific virtues we may or may not possess. Hence: the virtue of reason is prudence; the virtue of the will—or more precisely the spirited part of the soul—is fortitude; and the virtue of desire is moderation. Justice appears when all the parts work in the correct

---

[126] On the allegorical interpretation of the four stars, see C.S. Singleton, *Journey to Beatrice* (Baltimore: Johns Hopkins University Press, 1977), 159–183.

[127] In Jewish literature they appear in *4 Maccabees*, a work possibly written by Josephus.

order, when desire and will follow reason's lead (*Rep.*, 435b). So for the ancients, the virtuous person is not a walking head, nor are his feet up in the air. The rule is this: head first, feet follow.[128] Christianity early on adopted this structure of the four cardinal virtues.[129] The four stars in the early sky point to the aim of Dante's penance: recovery of the original holiness of Paradise. In the poem the garden is situated on the top of Mount Purgatory and signifies the practical end of diligent mortifications. But living in accordance with the four cardinal virtues, or what Aristotle and Aquinas will call "right reason," could hardly be sufficient. For one thing, St. Paul singled out not four virtues but three (cf. 1 Cor. 13:13). How do the new virtues relate to the old habits? Dante's literary solution illustrates the central Catholic principle that the supernatural never cancels the natural. Sometime after seeing the four stars, Dante notices the heavens again. The original four have set; three others now take their place:

> "What is it, son," my lord began to inquire,
> "That takes thine eye so?" "Those three torches there,"
> Said I, "that kindle all this pole with fire."

---

[128] In the medieval scholastic scheme Plato's tripartite soul is retained, although given a slightly more nuanced account. Reason (*intellectus*) remains, but will and desire become the rational and sensitive appetites (*appetites rationalis* and *appetites sensitivus*); for references see "Appetite" in *The Catholic Encyclopedia* (1907).

[129] A survey of the early adaptations of the Platonic schema by Ambrose, Jerome, Augustine, and Gregory the Great can be found in R. E. Houser's lengthy introduction to *The Cardinal Virtues: Aquinas, Albert, and Philip the Chancellor* (Toronto: Pontifical Institute of Mediaeval Studies, 2004), 32–37.

On Law

And he: "The four bright stars that shone so fair
To greet thee in the dawn have dipped from view
Yonder, and these have risen where they were.

(*Purg.*, cant. VIII, lines 88–93)

The rising of "those three torches" points to what the penitent can look to beyond Purgatory, to the theological virtues
of faith, hope, and charity. In theological terms, the cardinal
virtues remain even while their exercise is enhanced. As the
Catechism says, the theological virtues "give life" to all the
moral virtues; they "adapt man's faculties for participation in
the divine nature" (CCC 1813, 1812). So faith, hope, and
charity perfect reason, will, and desire. Knowledge of justice is
completed by Christ's fuller revelation of God's character, of his
mercy. The union of infinite justice with infinite mercy is what
St. John speaks of, for instance, when he writes that God is love
(cf. 1 John 4:16). The number of the stars is complete. In just
a few lines Dante has placed before our eyes the vast order of
the heavens, the arrangement of the virtues, and the goal of our
journey. Dante is not done climbing yet.

The mountain proper begins partway up, at St. Peter's Gate.
As the foundation of moral training is the right application of
pleasure and pain, to good habits must be added sound judgment. In other words, you cannot pass through the gate without
an exercise of *conscience*. Here marks our second lesson. Prior to
the gate the Christian walks up three steps, as Dante does in the
poem. The steps represent each of the parts of penance: confession, then contrition, and afterward satisfaction (*Purg.*, cant.
IX, lines 94–102). The scheme of the mountain, as of Christian morality more generally, presumes that men and women
are born with knowledge of good and evil. Every person has

some access to what philosophers from Thucydides and Cicero onward have called the natural law. In recent years the nature and value of natural-law theory as well as its position within Catholic moral theology has become the subject of much debate.[130] What is beyond dispute, however, is that natural law captures our access to right and wrong. The *Catechism* defines it this way.

> The natural law, present in the heart of each man and established by reason, is universal in its precepts and its authority extends to all men. It expresses the dignity of the person and determines the basis for his fundamental rights and duties. (CCC 1956)

What does law add to love? For one thing, the Church's recognition of natural law sets Catholic moral theology apart from fundamentalisms, religious and secular. It is also what adds justice to judgment. None can escape penance because none are without excuse. No doubt the application of this law has varied over time and according to place; and our knowledge of its precepts can be obscured through sin and base customs. Still, you do not need the Bible to tell you that killing innocents is wrong or that committing treason is shameful.

The seeds, even if not always the flowers, of justice are in some sense evident to all, however often we toss them aside. The three steps leading up to St. Peter's Gate signify the weight of obligation that freedom carries with it. Can man bear the load?

[130] Romanus Cessario, OP, provides a helpful orientation to recent debates surrounding natural-law theory in his *Introduction to Moral Theology* (Washington, DC: Catholic University of America Press), 68–77.

Here again we can measure the distance between our moral presuppositions and Dante's. Evidently, belief in natural law presumes the freedom of the will, the logical correlate of which is responsibility. Many of our contemporaries wonder whether the work of freedom is worth the bother, or even whether such a burden belongs to beasts such as ourselves. But, while we may question whether freedom is an illusion, Dante had no doubts. Within the *Purgatorio* Virgil eulogizes at length on the subject (cf. *Purg.*, cants. XVII–XVIII); in his epistle to *Cangrande* (13.25) Dante specifies the *Comedy*'s allegorical subject as follows: how "man, in the exercise of his free will, becomes liable to the rewards or punishments of justice."[131] The drama of the *Comedy*, and of the *Catechism* for that matter, depends upon this still small point. Without free will there is no responsibility; without responsibility the curtain is drawn. Neither comedy nor tragedy has any meaning in a world without freedom, since it would be a world without rules, a universe without risk. Wipe away human responsibility, and you might be able to construct a universe without losers, but you would have also rendered it a universe without players.

Already at the turn of the twentieth century, Hillaire Belloc (1870–1953) observed that Western democracies were devolving into "servile states"—political communities in which freedom was sold in exchange for material comfort.[132] In this instance the city truly is an image of the soul. Like the tail of a kite, the loss of political freedom trails closely behind the loss of personal freedom. And hasn't reason declared freedom illu-

---

[131] See discussion and citation in Warren Ginsberg's article "Free Will" in the *Dante Encyclopedia*, 425–427.

[132] See particularly Belloc's *The Servile State* (1913), introduction by R. Nisbet (Indianapolis: Liberty Classics, 1977).

sory anyway? If what many among the social-scientists tell is true, that man is the product of blind chance plus dumb matter, collective forces added to firing neurons, then choices really do not count. In such a scenario honest punishment vanishes too. As Evelyn Waugh so deliciously satirizes in his dystopian romance *Love among the Ruins* (1953), turn social-scientists into state-paid bureaucrats, and you abandon criminals to a far more punishing sentence than what less-enlightened ages meted out. Simply: therapy might not be a bad idea, but for some crimes punishment must come first. Otherwise you rob the criminal and the victim of their *human* dignity: you steal from them the mutual comfort of knowing that the act that came between them was *wrong*. The criminal with no guilt has no hope of forgiveness; the victim that suffered no ill-intent has no hope for vindication. The slide toward purely therapeutic approaches to criminal behavior is one more symptom of a nation's fall into decay, of the rule of soft tyranny, and of the renunciation of freedom.

Dante's lesson on moral responsibility is this: conscience *bears witness* to the natural law within; it testifies to law, it does not create it. In the poem this is represented by Dante's climb up to the gate. His first step, upon a stone of white marble, is an image of the Christian who peers into his conscience and owns his guilt. Honesty means admitting that all is not well within. The second, black stone, symbolizes mourning for sin. Not only must the pilgrim see his own fault; he must also be sorry for it—that is, desire not to do wrong again and to amend his ways. The last stone, representing the blood of Christ, and our blood, is red. Of this Pope John Paul II has written that suffering takes "salvific meaning," only when it is joined to the suffering of Christ (SD 1.1). As in *The Divine Comedy*, so also in the Church's fundamental moral teaching, in every act of penance three things must occur: we have to recognize that we have done wrong, regret the offense, and try to make up for the damage done (cf. CCC 1450–1460).

Dante has now nearly passed onto the first level of the mountain; but before he does there is one last detail to which we can attend. Dante confronts an angel with a brandished sword. The angel inscribes seven *P*s on the poet's head. The symbolism of the slash anticipates the division of the mountain as a whole.

> *Devoutly falling at the holy feet*
> *I prayed him let me in for mercy's sake,*
> *But first upon my breast three times I beat.*
>
> *Then did he write with his sword's point, and make*
> *Upon my brow the mark of seven P's;*
> *"Wash thou these wounds within there"; thus he spake.*
>
> (*Purg.*, cant. IX, lines 109–114)

The *P*s stand for the seven deadly sins (sin in Latin is *peccatum*). On each one of the seven cornices a particular vice will be wiped away: pride, envy, wrath, sloth, covetousness, gluttony, and lust.[133] Joining the other penitents, what does Dante

---

[133] There are, of course, innumerable details we are passing over. For one, the angel guarding the gate presents two keys, one gold, one silver. These signify the two parts of absolution that complete the act of penance, the absolution of sin and the distribution of a penance. The golden key, the costlier (*Purg.*, cant. IX, line 124), is the Church's authority to remit sin. This authority is, obviously, a derived authority, imparted to the Church by the infinite merits of Christ (CCC 1476). The other key points us to the function of the confessor. This is

see? After mounting an eighteen-foot-wide precipice Dante sees the penitent proud bent over with stones upon their backs and reciting the Lord's Prayer. As in every other cornice, penance consists in a submission to the opposite virtue. Those who were proud in the world are now doubled over, unable even to look Dante in the face (*Purg.*, cant. XI, line 54). With turned head what they can see are lifelike reliefs set along the side of the mountain wall.

As they make their slow round the penitents view examples of humility set in sculptured stone, of which Dante mentions three: the Blessed Virgin, King David, and the Emperor Trajan (*Purg.*, cant. X, lines 34–99). Each signifies a particular aspect of humility. Taken as a group the Mother of God, a Jew, and a Gentile illustrate the way that knowledge of virtue has been available to people living during each stage of salvation history—after, during, and before the Mosaic law. They see something on the ground too. Beneath their feet are inscribed lifelike images of pride. Three groups of deterrent examples correspond to the three images of humility seen in sculpture (*Purg.*, cant. XII, lines 25–66): Lucifer contrasts with the trust of Mary; Saul

---

where skill is required on the part of the priest. As the *Catechism* relates, in selecting a fitting penance, the confessor "must take into account the penitent's personal situation" (CCC 1460). That means a confessor should discern the causes that led the penitent into sin in the first place—which of the seven deadly sins lay at the root of this or that particular faulty behavior. Good confessors are always in demand. Everyone wants to see them because, like Fr. Brown of Chesterton's detective series, the master confessor is the master of human motivations. He is able to see how our individual failings fall along one of the other common fault lines that can run through the human heart.

stands against the joyful self-forgetfulness of David; and Cyrus, king of the Persians, is set opposite of the generous Trajan, who is remembered for his gift to a poor widow.[134] Lastly, each cornice includes a prayer, a benediction, and a greeting from an angel that will brush away one *P* from the forehead of the penitent. There are seven such cornices. Dante's steps grow lighter as he scrambles up to the next one (*Purg.*, cant. XII, line 116).

Observing the organization of these cornices we come to our third and fourth lessons. On the structure of the mountain, Virgil offers his famous discourse in Canto 17:

> *"Love of the Good," said he, "that once let slide*
> *Its proper duties, is restored up there;*
> *There once again the slackened oar is plied.*
>
> *But if [love] swerve to evil, or pursue*
> *Good ends too hot of foot or slack of speed,*
> *Then the Workman's work His work undo.*
>
> *Bethink thee then how love must be the seed*
> *In you, not only of each virtuous action,*
> *But also of each punishable deed.*
> (*Purg.*, cant. XVII, lines 85–88, 100–105)

The rationale for the division of the mountain is derived most directly, of course, from St. Thomas Aquinas.[135] But

---

[134] On this see further D. Sayers notes to canto XII, p. 162.

[135] On this see E. Gilson's *Dante and Philosophy*, trans. D. Moore (New York: Harper Torchbooks, 1963); for a recent commentary that is more attentive to the Augustinian themes in the poem see R. Martinez and R. Durling's *The Divine Comedy of Dante Alighieri: Vol. 2: Purgatorio* (Oxford: Oxford University Press, 2003).

behind and along with him the two earlier sources are Aristotle and St. Augustine.

Dante's adaptation of Aristotle locates our third lesson. Upon each cornice one of the deadly sins is purged, while one opposing virtue is taken on.[136] But what, precisely, defines a vice? What marks our misstep in love? In the *Purgatorio* Dante has his guide Virgil specify three possibilities: Love can either (a) pursue the wrong object, "swerve to evil," or (b) pursue a good at "too hot" a speed, or (c) at a pace too "slack." Virgil's explanation calls to mind Aristotle's doctrine formulated in the *Nichomachean Ethics*: "By virtue I mean virtue of character; for this is about feelings and actions, and these admit of excess, deficiency, and an intermediate condition" (1106b).[137] For Dante, following Aristotle, the virtuous person acts and feels according to the rule of *the mean*. Bravery, in this scheme, stands at the midpoint between cowardice and rashness. The geography of the mountain offers a visual representation of this doctrine. Lower Purgatory purges vices caused by choosing the wrong object. Middle and Upper Purgatory purge vices that are

---

[136] As the *Catechism* notes, there are at least two ways that vices can be categorized. They "can be classified according to the virtues they oppose or also be linked to the capital sins which Christian experience has distinguished" (CCC 1866). The classification used by Dante is according to the seven deadly sins. The seven vices of the *Purgatorio* are the seven chief sins that, through repetition, have become habits (cf. CCC 1876).

[137] Aristotle's text continues: "But having these feelings at the right times, about the right things, toward the right people, for the right end, and in the right way, is the intermediate and best condition, and this is proper to virtue. Similarly, actions also admit of excess, deficiency, and an intermediate condition" (trans. T. Irwin, second edition [Indianapolis: Hackett Publishing Company, 1999]).

Our Lady of Perpetual Help Chapel, Walsh University, Ohio

caused by choosing the right object in the wrong way. Within this unity, the seven cornices thus fall within three groups: vices that are the result of love perverted (pride, envy, wrath); vice that is the result of love defective (sloth); and vices that are the result of love excessively directed toward created goods (covetousness, gluttony, lust).[138] Our third lesson: we violate the principle of the mean whenever we choose secondary goods in a defective or excessive manner.

Dante takes from St. Augustine our final lesson: both vice and virtue spring from love. Mount Purgatory rises up according to the *ordo amoris*, the order of love. In Augustine's attempt to draw together Plato with St. Paul, he recognized that any Christian synthesis must accept the primacy of charity. Early in his career he sought a unifying principle among the virtues

[138] On this the reader is directed to the helpful diagrams in the Dorothy Sayers edition of *Purgatory*, 62, 202–203.

identified by Plato. After his conversion, he came to see that St. Paul had already discovered it: Christ crucified, in divine love. Fusing St. Paul with Plato St. Augustine proposed that prudence, fortitude, temperance, and justice could all be described as four *forms* of love directed toward our final end. So he writes: "As to virtue leading us to the happy life, I hold virtue to be nothing else than perfect love of God." Accordingly, prudence is love understanding the means to God; fortitude is love bearing all hardships for the sake of God; temperance is love keeping ourselves pure for God; and justice is love rendering service to God (*On the Morals of the Catholic Church*, 15.25).[139] The primacy of love is affirmed in the *Catechism* as well when it concludes that the "practice of all the virtues is animated and inspired by charity" (CCC 1827).

Conclusion

Dante's organization of Mount Purgatory recommends itself not only because of its beauty but also because of the clarity with which his images synthesize classical and biblical traditions of moral philosophy. Simply by looking at the poem's structure we learn four lessons central to the Catholic moral

---

[139] "As to virtue leading us to the happy life, I hold virtue to be nothing else than perfect love of God. For the fourfold division of virtue I regard as taken from four forms of love. For these virtues ...I should have no hesitation in defining them: that temperance is love giving itself entirely to that which is loved; fortitude is love readily bearing all things for the sake of the loved object, therefore ruling rightly; prudence is love distinguishing with sagacity between what hinders it and what helps it. The object of this love in not anything, but only God, the chief good, the highest wisdom, the perfect harmony" (trans. Stothert, p.48).

vision: (1) the pedagogical value of pleasure and pain; (2) the witness of conscience to the natural law; (3) the doctrine of the mean; (4) and the primacy of love. Because virtue presupposes natural law, there can be no Christianity apart from law. Obedience requires more than that we be born again; it calls us even to be transformed into the likeness of Christ, literally to become perfect icons. It is sometimes said that Catholic morality, especially sexual morality, takes a gloomy view of the human condition, that it is afraid of pleasure and obsessed with sin. Some who do not enjoy Dante cite such reasons. I think their reason lies elsewhere. Dante is unlike the modern poets not because his images of Hell are grotesque. Dante is unlike the modern poets because he is cheery and we are glum. If the pageantry and music of *The Divine Comedy* appears childlike it is because we find it hard to believe that grown-up creatures like ourselves could really be so, well, happy. The moralism that most poisons us today is not of the sort that cannot lift its eyes from the letter of the law, but the moralism of the herd, of those who simply cannot be bothered to become excellent. Above all, what the *Comedy* teaches us about the Christian life and the renewal of Catholic culture is that there is no perfection apart from penance. This is why, if we hope for Heaven, even earth must be a prelude to Purgatory.

The Presentation of the Lord, Michael D. O'Brien

7

On the Family:
How Love Grows

The first school of prayer

Childhood images of prayer remain for life. In her autobiography St. Thérèse of Lisieux offers an intimate portrait of the making of a saint. Although her family would suffer severe losses, the days and weeks of her childhood were enveloped in prayer.

> Every afternoon I used to go for a walk with Papa, and we made our visit to the Blessed Sacrament together. We used to go round all the churches in turn, and that's how I had my first experience of going into the chapel at Carmel. There, Papa shewed me the grille that shuts off the choir, and told me that there were nuns beyond it; the suspicion never crossed my mind that nine years later I should be one of them.

The joy of Sunday impressed itself vividly upon her young imagination:

> Big feasts, of course, only came now and then, but every week brought one feast to which I had a real devotion—Sunday. There was nothing like Sunday, God's

own holiday, the day of rest.... All the way to Church, and even when we'd got into Church, Papa let the little princess hold his hand; my place was next to him, and when we had to go down into the body of the Church for the sermon, two chairs must be found side by side.[140]

Pope Benedict XVI has likewise spoken of the impression that Corpus Christi processions made on him while a young boy in Bavaria:

I can still smell the carpets of flowers and the freshness of the birch trees; I can recall the decorations on all the houses, the banners, the singing; I can still hear the village band, which, on this occasion, sometimes even ventured more than it could! I can hear the firing of guns by which the local youth celebrated their own *joie de vivre* while, at the same time, saluting Christ as a head of state, as the Head of State, the Lord of the world, and welcoming him to their streets and into their village. The perpetual presence of Christ was celebrated on this day as though it were a state visit in which not even the smallest village was forgotten.[141]

The silent background of such memories is most often the faith of parents. Without the memory of prayer in the domestic Church few find their home in the pew as adults. In recent times there have arisen many hopeful signs of rejuvenation in teaching on the family (one thinks, for instance, of the enormous

---

[140] Thérèse of Lisieux, *The Story of the Soul*, trans. Ronald Knox (London: The Harvill Press, 1958), 59, 65.

[141] Cited in Rowland, *Ratzinger's Faith*, 135; taken from the collection of Ratzinger's writings, *Co-Workers of the Truth* (San Francisco: Ignatius Press, 1992), 134–135.

On the Family

Corpus Christi procession, Oxford, United Kingdom

success of Marriage Encounter Ministries in North America), but even the most casual acquaintance with the status of the family in industrial nations should be enough to place marriage preparation at the top of every bishop's priority list for his diocese.

Leo Tolstoy's *Anna Karenina* opens: "Happy families are all alike; every unhappy family is unhappy in its own way."[142] Never has so fine a novel begun with so flawed a premise. In real life happy families are infinitely more varied and interesting than unhappy ones. To walk into a loving home is to enter the kingdom of a vast and spacious realm. In an unhappy home, no matter how large the floor plan, there is never enough

---

[142] Leo Tolstoy, *Anna Karenina*, trans. Constance Garnett (New York: The Bobbs-Merrill Co., 1978), 1.

room. Monotony reigns. Variation ebbs and flows not with the turn of fasts and feasts but according to the predictable round of conflict and indifference. It is possible for an intact statue to be unique; it is the mess of clay and shattered glass that is common. Contra Tolstoy, the happy home is the true work of art. What Pope Leo XIII initiated for workers at the end of the nineteenth century, John Paul II did for marriage and the family at the end of the twentieth. Both through his Theology of the Body and in his Apostolic Exhortation *Familiaris Consortio* (1981) the late pontiff outlined a program for the renewal of the family in the modern world. What is now obvious is that if family is to thrive as a school of prayer and as a seedbed for mysticism, then marriage catechesis will have to serve up more than the usual gruel of budget tips and friendly advice typically offered in parish preparation programs.

There is a mountain of social scientific study that has been tracking the deleterious effects that divorce has on couples, on their children, and on society. To mention a sample among the waning vital signs I note, to begin with, that fewer people bother to get married at all. In both Canada and the United States, for instance, the marriage rate has dropped 50 percent over the past fifty years (due mostly to cohabitation).[143] When

---

[143] In the United States during 2001 there were 45.6 marriages per thousand unmarried women ages 15 and older compared with 90.2 in 1950. For studies see *The Family Portrait: A Compilation of Data, Research and Public Opinion on the Family*, 2nd ed., ed. Bridget Maher (Washington, DC: The Family Research Council, 2004). And, drawing upon slightly different metric, in Canada in 2006 there were 4.7 marriages for every thousand people (that figure is 2.8 in Quebec) compared with 10.9 in the 1940s. See "Marriages" in *The Daily*, January 17, 2007, a publication of Statistics Canada.

men and women do marry, it is not as high school sweethearts but as professionals. Thus in 2002 the average age at first marriage for men in the United States was 26.9 years (compared with 23.2 in 1970), 25.3 for women (compared with 20.8 in 1970).[144] Once married your chance of divorcing is about 50 percent. That figure, of course, does not apply if you use Natural Family Planning: only 1 to 3 percent of such couples divorce; but then, there are not many of those couples.[145] All of this is dreary enough. Worse is what such figures presage for the future. With fewer couples getting married, we also have fewer children than did our grandparents' generation. So adverse have we become to babies that not a single European country can claim a replacement birthrate. Germany, Greece, Italy, and Spain all hover around 1.3 live births per women. American women have about 2.1 children, while Canadians have 1.58 (2.1 per women is the minimum birthrate to maintain a replacement population rate).[146] It may sound fine to have fewer people to have to bump into at the grocery store, but the real costs are dramatic: economic stagnation, dependence upon immigration, and ultimately cultural suicide. As the Pontifical Council for the Family's *Declaration on the Decrease of Fertility in the World*

[144] See *The Family Portrait*, 3. Canadians marry later. According to the 2006 census the average age for first-time grooms was 30.6, and brides 28.5 (compared with 25.2 years for men and 22.8 years for women in 1973). See "Marriages" in *The Daily*, January 17, 2007.

[145] See studies cited in R. Wetzel's *Sexual Wisdom: A Guide for Parents, Young Adults, Educators and Physicians* (Huntington Beach, California: Sex Education for Advanced Beginners, 1998), 108.

[146] According to the recent figures released by the Population Reference Bureau and which can be accessed through their website, www.prb.org.

(1998) noted, decreased fertility is a mark of cultural pessimism. The political stability of a nation requires families who produce children.

If nations require parents, boys and girls need dads who will tuck them in at night. In 1960 a mere 5 percent of children were born out of wedlock; by 1995 that percentage had rocketed to 32; the U.S. Centers for Disease Control and Prevention recently reported that births to unmarried women now account for 39.7 percent of all children.[147] That means a lot of broken hearts. It also means a lot of prison terms. There is no other single factor that contributes to a child's performance in school, his ability to stay out of jail, and his capacity for future marriage more than whether or not he has a father who comes home at night.[148] Clearly, if the Church is to fulfill her mission as the sacrament of salvation in the world, the family as the first transmitter of faith must function, and function well. Much of what has been said in previous chapters about the educating power of architecture, of tradition, and of Christology comes to look rather beside the point when nearly a majority of children no longer have two parents who can take them to church. For a generation of young people who have had the memory of an intact family wiped away, John Paul II's writings on the mission of the family have taken on a particular urgency.

[147] Statistics from 1960 and 1995 in David Popenoe's "Life without Father," in *Lost Fathers: The Politics of Fatherlessness in America*, ed. Cynthia R. Daniels (New York: St. Martin's Griffin Press, 2000), 34; the 2009 findings reported in "Why Marriage Matters" by Caitlin Flanagan, in *Time*, July 13, 2009, 45–49.

[148] See studies cited in *The Family Portrait*, 20–23, *Fatherless America: Confronting Our Most Urgent Social Problem* (New York: Basic Books, 1995) and Daniels, *Lost Fathers*.

On the Family

* * *

We have now arrived at the *Catechism*'s final division. From the precepts of Christian morality we turn to the *Catechism*'s fourth part, on prayer.[149] Prayer and the cultivation of an interior communion with God is what animate the faith, worship, and discipleship of each believer. As the patron of moral theologians, St. Alphonsus Liguori, wrote: "Those who pray are certainly saved; those who do not pray are certainly damned" (cf. CCC 2744).

Catholic culture is the fruit of saints at work in the world, and there are no saints without prayer. Where do they learn their lessons? While there are many guides to prayer (priests, monks and nuns, friends, etc.), the *Catechism* specifies the *family* as "the first place of education in prayer" (CCC 2685). In other words, mysticism begins with Mom and Dad. Accordingly, in this chapter we are concerned not so much with the fruits of mysticism as with their roots in childhood and in the disciplines of the family. In a particularly dark age in our cultural history—let us say, between the seventh and tenth centuries—it was monks and nuns that preserved Christian culture for a future age. Once again darkness envelops. This time it will not primarily be the monasteries that preserve the habits of Christian culture; it will

---

[149] The *Catechism* describes the order among the parts this way: "'Great is the mystery of the faith!' The Church professes this mystery in the Apostles' Creed (Part One) and celebrates it in the sacramental liturgy (Part Two), so that the life of the faithful may be conformed to Christ in the Holy Spirit to the glory of God the Father (Part Three). This mystery, then, requires that the faithful believe in it, that they celebrate it, and that they live from it in a vital and personal relationship with the living and true God. This relationship is prayer" (CCC 2558).

be families. Renewing the spirit of holiness among Catholics requires, of necessity, the revitalization of the family. To see how the family can serve as a school of prayer we will reflect first on its mission and then also on its enemies.

John Paul II on the mission of the family

The supernatural builds upon the natural. So also there must be a dinner on the table before grace can be said over it. In his charter on the Christian family in the modern world *Familiaris Consortio*, John Paul II outlined four functions that the mission of the family comprises: forming a community of persons, serving life, contributing to society, and sharing in the work of the Church. Restoring the health of the hearth in our time requires not only enacting the domestic virtues suitable to each of these functions (which is no small achievement), but also identifying the ideas and institutions that undermine them.

As a *community of persons* the family is founded upon, first, the faithful love of a man and woman (FC 18-27). As Alice von Hildebrand wrote to a young bride, although requiring unmeasured sacrifices, "a great love between husband and wife can also be the deepest source of happiness this side of heaven."[150] Christians have in this sense nearly always appeared Romantic about the possibilities of nuptial joy. As the second-century Tertullian wrote:

How can I ever express the happiness of a marriage joined by the Church?... How wonderful the bond between two believers, now one in hope, one in desire, one in discipline, one in the same service! They are both

[150] Alice von Hildebrand, *By Love Refined* (Manchester, New Hampshire: Sophia Institute Press, 1989), 4.

Family bike ride in the country

children of the one Father and servants of the same Master, undivided in spirit and flesh, truly two in one flesh. Where the flesh is one, one also is the spirit. (*Ad uxorem* 2.7.6–7; CCC 1642)

But if Christians are romantics, their high hopes are rooted in the earth. Marital happiness is possible only when the nature of the union is respected. The domestic Church constitutes a communion of persons when, established in love, it enacts the disciplines characteristic of this union—fidelity, work, forgiveness, catechesis (cf. CCC 1657). Of course, sanctity is the goal of all baptized Christians. Nevertheless, when two become one, the means to that universal vocation takes on a designated shape. Man and woman are equally called to serve each other in Christ, yet that basic equality does not efface either the *form* that marriage takes or the *differences* between men and women that the union presumes. Those differences which allow for interdependence and specialization within marriage are rooted in, although by no means limited to, biology. In common do the husband and wife seek the virtues; but only as man and woman are virtues draped in flesh and blood. Like the two sides of a magnet, the complementary composition of the sexes builds strength within the marriage bond. And it is from this position of strength that a family is capable to extend itself outward to the elderly, to strangers, and most of all, to children.

This leads to the second role, *serving life* (FC 28-41). In hindsight it was not difficult to predict, as Pope Paul VI did, that once the marital act was detached from having children, sex would lose its seriousness, as it now has for many disillusioned young. On the inversion of the purpose of sexual appetite Canadian political philosopher George Grant once commented:

> The modern union of individuality and materialism has meant a transposition of older beliefs about the relation of sex and love. In the older beliefs sexual desire was one means through which love between human beings could abound; in our era love seems sometimes to be thought of as a means for the abounding of sexual enjoyment.[151]

As bitter experience has now proven, the sexual revolution did not liberate eros; it only drained it of its energies. The Church has never been opposed to eros even if at times she warns us of it. Eros is that love which compels men and women to seek what is outside, what is unknown. It drives our

[151] George Grant, "Faith and the Multiversity," in *Technology and Justice* (Concord, Ontario: House of Anansi Press, 1986), 51–52.

explorations; it is the electric arc that draws lovers into their first kiss, no less than it is the passion that fuels the first Latin lesson. But if you are going to master the grammar and get to the pleasure of reading what lies between the pages, you will have to be led by more than the love of novelty. You will also need to learn the habits of loyalty, of fairness, and of self-sacrifice.[152]

All great explorations require the explosive force it takes to make a beginning. But setting out to sea and arriving safely into port are not the same things: nor do they merit the same honors. The (male) lover guided solely by eros condemns himself only to a thousand false starts. Besides never reaching his destination, unlike a real man, he never truly exposes himself to danger. The shore-hugging traveler cannot experience the thrill of sailing upon the high seas, of navigating waters far beyond the point of no return. The marauder, the metrosexual, the free spirit liberated from chastity, turns out after all to be merely a frightened boy chained to his adolescence.

Once upon a time, marriage used to save eros from ruin. A primary aim of marriage was to channel the explosive energies of eros in the service of love and of life. For those who remained faithful, to the victors who followed eros all the way into marriage, nature offered her own laurel wreath: children.

The third function of the family is its *service to society* (FC 42-48). Here John Paul emphasized the political and economic dimensions of the family. Nations are built of cities, cities of neighborhoods, and neighborhoods of households. The

---

[152] In Greek loyalty is roughly *storge* (familial love), fairness *philia* (friendship love), and self-sacrifice *agape* (divine love); these, along with eros, make up the four kinds of love distinguished by classical Greek and the subject of C. S. Lewis's delightful study *The Four Loves* (London: Collins, 1982).

integrity of households depends on the chastity of spouses. Modesty is the guardian of chastity, as every Jane Austen novel will teach you. Keeping one's virginity is the best way to save eros from being spoiled.[153] Endless chatter about social justice without restoring modesty in our society is a little bit like a call for cleaner decks on the *Titanic*. If you want justice among nations, build tranquility among spouses. If the family is under siege, so is society. Man is social. Between the individual and the state lie the innumerable and overlapping forms of community life that constitute our lives (hockey clubs, business associations, learned societies, knitting circles) (cf. RN 73). At the basis of these and prior to them all is the family. Staring into the threats to the modern family, the fathers of the Second Vatican Council stated: "Since the Creator of all things has established the conjugal partnership as the beginning and basis of human society" the family is "the first and vital cell of society" (AA 11, cited in FC 42). Peace does literally begin at home. As family unravels, so with it does every other association; and, predictably enough, government expands to fill in the missing spaces. So in communism all are absorbed in the collective while in liberal capitalism the individual is isolated and left exposed; in both, humanity is under attack.

That community which is the universal destiny of redeemed humanity is, of course, not the state, nor even the family. It is the City of God, the Church. Family is a great good, but its

---

[153] For one young Jewish woman's discovery of this lost virtue see Wendy Shalit, *A Return to Modesty: Discovering the Lost Virtue* (Toronto: HarperCollins, 1999) and *Girls Gone Mild: Young Women Reclaim Self-Respect and Find It's Not Bad to Be Good* (New York: Random House, 2007); on the social and private costs of losing our innocence see Mary Eberstadt's lead article "The Weight of Smut" in *First Things* (June/July 2010).

claims are penultimate. The fourth function of family, and the one that touches most directly on the topic of prayer, is its task to serve the *mission of the Church* (FC 49-64). A family accomplishes this function when it acts as a school of prayer for its members.

The family lives of St. Thérèse and Pope Benedict XVI show that being rooted in the traditions of a particular family need not close you off from others. To the contrary, boys and girls learn best how to thrive in a large kingdom if they have first been loved within a small one. Our Lord promises, "For where two or three are gathered together in my name, there I am in the midst of them" (Matt. 18:20). It is typically through the rhythms of family prayer that we are opened up to the universal prayer of the Church. As John Paul II argued, "an important purpose of prayer in the domestic Church is to serve as the natural introduction for the children to the liturgical prayer of the whole Church" (FC 61). Thus, the Rosary, the Divine Office, meditation on the word of God, devotions to the Sacred Heart of Jesus and the Immaculate Heart of Mary, grace before meals, and such forms of prayer help the family "strive to celebrate at home, and in a way suited to the members, the times and feasts of the liturgical year" (FC 61). With pastoral insight John Paul II noted how it is the parents' own witness that will most count in the eyes of children.

> The concrete example and living witness of parents is fundamental and irreplaceable in educating their children to prayer. Only by praying together with their children can a father and mother—exercising their royal priesthood [i.e., rightful authority]—penetrate the innermost depths of their children's hearts and leave an

impression that the future events of their lives will not be able to efface. (FC 60)

The family's ability to perform each of these functions will to a considerable extent dictate the Church's success in renewing Catholic culture in our time. Families are always imperfect. Parents can cooperate with grace only in a spirit of dependence, knowing that all our frail efforts must be entrusted to the mercy of God. Raising children is hard work. Our historical situation has only complicated that task. Perhaps for the first time in our cultural history the very *idea* of the family is under attack. Young people accordingly need to acquire not only the virtues of domesticity but the intellectual and moral nerve to counter those ideas and institutions that work against the purposes of the family. Some of these are worth singling out.

The Ecclesia domestica and its despisers

The masters of social media have long perpetuated prejudices against the family that, unchallenged, lead to its ruin. Among the several we could cite, here are three: (1) the assertion that marriage makes men and women less free; (2) the assumption that children are a burden; and (3) the insistence that sexual differentiation is a fiction. These three ideas represent, as it were, three waves of the anti-family movement of the past 150 years. The first is the Marxist contribution; the second is the eugenicist; the third is the fruit of recent gender theorists.

Common to both Marx and Engels is the belief that social relations not characterized by strict material equality are unjust. In his influential study, *The Origin of the Family, Private Property, and the State* (1884), Karl Marx's collaborator Friedrich Engels attacked the family as the original cell of inequality and slavery.

The Alba Madonna, Raphael, Italian, c. 1510, oil on panel

As an extension of man's first desire for property—Marxism's equivalent of the fall—man also wished to secure the transmission of property to his posterity. In Engels' account this drive is what gives rise to monogamy. Men with land want heirs with legitimate title. Hence, in marriage women belong to men simply "as an instrument for the production of children."[154] In Engels' view the enslavement of women, naturally, like all

[154] Friedrich Engels, *The Origin of the Family, Private Property, and the State* (New York: International Publishers, 1970), 50.

inequalities, will cease once the means of production are transferred from private ownership to the state. With no right to property and no possibility of handing on an inheritance, men will no longer care to identify their offspring. An upshot is that once the economic conditions that gave rise to marriage cease, so also will marriage. At the end of history, sex will again be unfettered. Engels predicted that the coming revolution would strike a blow to both family and the bourgeois sexual morality that sustained it. In the socialist future, "the single family ceases to be the economic unit of society," which will result in "the gradual growth of unconstrained sexual intercourse."[155] Evidently, Freud was not the first to suggest that sex is what people are really after.

Whatever the defects of his theory, Engels was prescient at least about its ramifications: as socialism advances, family recedes. As the tasks of raising children, caring for the old, and making money are absorbed by the state, fewer and fewer reasons will remain for a man and a woman to form a lasting bond. In my travels in former communist countries I have been struck by how closely our attitude toward the education of children matched communist methods. There is this difference, however: under communism millions of mothers were forced to work out of the home and send their children to state institutions. In the free world many of us do this of our own accord.

When children from the age of three years spend two or more meals with strangers, it is not surprising that parents find it difficult to command the level of loyalty that was once taken for granted. More than "quality time" young children need quantities of time, and when the home is vacant, children

---

[155] Engels, *The Origin of the Family*, 67.

transfer their allegiances elsewhere, usually to their peers. Boys and girls exposed early to state institutions become easy prey to what has been called "youth culture"—that sum of the popular music, expensive clothing, and crass entertainments devised by corporations to provide an easy market. When Mom is at work, parenting becomes more difficult too. In fact, the demands of work can come to look fun when set beside parenthood. For more and more parents, the sacrifices at home appear to offer a meager return. Certainly some young mothers have no choice but to work outside the home; but the need is hardly the norm. The household has to be more than just a bus terminal where connections to other destinations are made. It has to return to being a center for meaningful *activity*. Education, work, prayer, nurture, and play are all essential functions belonging to the household properly ordered. Restoring the strength of the single-unit family turns on its ability, then, as Aidan Nichols has observed, "to recover ground from the exterior agencies to whom too many of its tasks have too often been transferred."[156]

Writing a generation after Marx and Engels, Pope Leo XIII understood well what was at stake in the fight against socialism. *Rerum Novarum* (1891) had in view not only the rights of the worker but also the survival of his family. Both have rights that are grounded in nature and disclosed by revelation: "Behold, therefore, the family, or rather the society of the household, a very small society indeed, but a true one, and older than any polity!" (RN 19). The indignation of couples needs to be aroused at the present danger that confronts their happiness. Equality and complementarity can in fact coexist in happy union. The Christian simply does not need to accept that equality must (as

[156] Nichols, *Christendom Awake*, 93.

in Marixist terms) be reduced to wage parity and equal opportunity for sexual license. In this first wave of attack on the family, any sign of mutual interdependence was viewed as a threat to freedom. Those working against the family have insisted that submission to an exclusive contract is a sacrifice of autonomy. As Simone de Beauvoir claimed, in marriage, "man and wife together undergo the oppression of an institution they did not create."[157]

Needless to say, the oppression under which men and women suffer most is not the result of marriage but of broken promises. Even by such pedestrian indexes as wealth, health, and reported happiness, a mountain of social-scientific research has long overturned the popular wisdom of such 1960s thrillers as *The Second Sex* and Betty Friedman's *The Feminine Mystique*. Like men, women simply thrive better in marriage. They suffer less depression, are more financially secure, and experience more fulfilling intimacy. Even today, after decades of assault on the ideal of the nuclear family, a mere 8 percent of women say they hope to remain unwed.[158]

The second wave also accepted the Marxist premise that justice demands strict material equality. Next the wagging finger turned from men to *children*. If women wish to have sex with men, they should not be punished with unwanted offspring.

---

[157] Simone de Beauvoir, *The Second Sex* [1949], trans. and ed. H.M. Parshley (New York: Bantam Books, 1961), 454.

[158] Many of these statistics are conveniently compiled in L.J. Waite and M. Gallagher, *The Case for Marriage: Why Married People are Happier, Healthier, and Better Off Financially* (New York: Doubleday, 2000): on married women's greater mental health see p. 166; on their greater wealth, and enjoyment of physical intimacy see p.170; on how many consider singleness versus marriage as an ideal see p. 3.

A few students among the hundreds of thousands
at the Washington, DC, March for Life

For the most part, artificial contraception was seen as the first
ring of defense, but from the beginning, abortion was always
the backup. The connection between contraception, economic
equality, and access to abortion was made public in 1992 by the
United States Supreme Court ruling on *Planned Parenthood v.
Casey,* which upheld the prior 1973 decision in favor of abortion in *Roe v. Wade* in these memorable words:

> The Roe rule's limitation on state power could not be
> repudiated without serious inequity to people who, for
> two decades of economic and social developments,
> have organized intimate relationships and made choices
> that define their views of themselves and their places
> in society, in reliance on the availability of abortion in

the event that contraception should fail. The ability of women to participate equally in the economic and social life of the Nation has been facilitated by their ability to control their reproductive lives.[159]

Tolerance of legalized abortion is the gravest consequence that follows once you accept contraception, but it is not the only one. In 1930 the Anglican Communion became the first Christian group to approve of the use of artificial contraception. And following from this, Archbishop of Canterbury Rowan Williams also notes (approvingly) that to say yes to the condom is to lose the right to condemn sodomy. Separate sex from procreation, and homosexual unions become equivalent to heterosexual ones. To this end Williams has concluded:

> In a church that accepts the legitimacy of contraception, the absolute condemnation of same-sex relations of intimacy must rely either on an abstract fundamentalist deployment of a number of very ambiguous biblical texts, or on a problematic and nonscriptural theory about natural complementarity, applied narrowly and crudely to physical differentiation without regard to psychological structures.[160]

The logic of the archbishop is sound, of course—so long as you accept the premise. Within a church that accepts contraception, censuring gay unions is arbitrary. Although Roman Catholics now stand alone as the only Christian body that

---

[159] United States Supreme Court, *Planned Parenthood v. Casey* (1992), 505, U.S. 833 (pp. 855–856).

[160] "The Body's Grace," in *Theology and Sexuality*, ed. Eugene F. Rogers, Jr. (Oxford: Blackwell, 2002), 320.

unequivocally rejects artificial contraception, prior to 1930 every Christian body—and many other religious groups—opposed it as an affront to human dignity. The temporary or permanent sterilization of a healthy man or women not only degrades the conjugal act; it undermines the union as such. As Mahatma Gandhi warned in 1925, "I urge the advocates of artificial methods of birth control to consider the consequences. Any large use of the methods is likely to result in the dissolution in the marriage bond."[161]

In any event, the eugenicist and anti-natal movement popularized by Margaret Sanger (1879–1966) and perpetuated through Planned Parenthood has been so overwhelmingly successful that great effort will be required to awaken the imaginations of the young to a world where children are not viewed as a social and economic burden. What atonement will be required for the holocaust of our little ones is difficult to imagine. Beyond searing our own consciences, we have only now begun to suffer the social costs of killing. Europe has entered its demographic winter; what China will experience once the full effect of wiping out a generation of girls is felt, one can hardly guess.[162]

Having turned first against men, and then against children, today the assault on the family directly targets *women*. It is from the third wave that the more bizarre claims about the sexes are being trumpeted, and the most bizarre claim of all is that sex

[161] Quoted in Wetzel, *Sexual Wisdom*, 108.

[162] See the March 4, 2010, lead article in *The Economist*, "Gendercide: Killed, Aborted or Neglected, At Least 100 Million Girls Have Disappeared—and the Number Is Rising." Surprising as it is that this bastion of liberal secular opinion should even raise the problem, readers were assured that, while the journal objects to discriminating between boys and girls, it has no objection to equal opportunity in the womb.

is illusory. For a generation, college freshman have learned to blink obediently when told that "gender" is a social construction. The term *gender* does refer to a social construct. But only words can have masculine, feminine, or even neuter gender: human beings have male or female sex. Feminists (and many Christians) used to argue for women's suffrage on the grounds that men and women share a common nature. Now they claim a distinctly feminine irrationality and implicitly deny a common human nature.

On this score the leading edge of the feminist movement has traveled vast distances since Mary Wollstonecraft's *A Vindication of the Rights of Women* (1792). By and large, feminists today have repositioned the basis of their claims to follow the latest fashions of postmodern philosophy. Thus, Luce Irigaray defends women's privileged status not on the foundation of reason but on the basis of its denial. To cite just one example, in her work *This Sex Which Is Not One* we learn that: "Hers are contradictory words, somewhat mad from the standpoint of reason, inaudible to whoever listens to them with ready-made grids, with a fully elaborated code in hand."[163] Whatever the author might wish to affirm, she appears to deny women their share in a common rationality. This is most unfortunate. For one thing, without participating in reason, there is little on which to base the principle of equality between the sexes. Likewise, arguing that women participate in different "rationalities" can serve only to decrease women's happiness—since most desire to share in some sort of friendship with men. A world in which men and women do not share a universal reason might make some lesbians feel more at home; but it would be

---

[163] *This Sex Which Is Not One*, trans. C. Porter (Ithaca, New York: Cornell University Press, 1985), 29.

a much smaller world to enjoy, without meaningful friendship between sisters and brothers, wives and husbands, mothers and their sons. (Irigaray at least seems to believe that a women's happiness is better served apart from the family.) Not willing to be pigeonholed by the ready-made labels of hetero-homo or transsexual identities, Irigaray proposes what has been termed "polymorphous sensuality."[164] Building public washrooms will never be the same.

What are we to make of such waves? Frequently, at the root of these attacks on family lies a corruption of what John Paul II has called "the idea and the experience of freedom." In the late pope's analysis, underlying these ideas and the social and economic institutions supporting them is a notion of freedom conceived not as a capacity for realizing truth, "but as an autonomous power of self-affirmation" (FC 6). In place of such a notion, and enacted through the disciplines and habits suitable for family, man and woman united in matrimony are called to embody the self-giving love of Christ. There can hardly be a more attractive witness of self-giving love than a family at prayer.

The family at prayer

The *Catechism* draws attention to the patterns of prayer revealed through the lives of Old Testament saints from Abraham to Moses to David. These represent in turn the intercessor,

---

[164] On this description of Irigaray's project see Elaine Storkey's *Origins of Difference* (Grand Rapids, Michigan: Baker Academic, 2001), 59. Like many other postmodern philosophers, Irigaray's work is often riddled with jargon, non sequiturs, and nonsense that is scrutinized in works such as Alan Sokal and Jean Bricmont's *Intellectual Impostures: Postmodern Philosophers' Abuse of Science* (London: Profile Books, 1998), 97–113.

the contemplative, and the lover (cf. CCC 2570–2580).[165] Needless to say, in the rehabilitation of the family, including the family at prayer, Christians will need to relearn the disciplines of domesticity even as they regain the tools to defend the family in speech.

Throughout the twentieth century there has been a renewal of thinking about the vocation of the family, including thinking about the role of women.[166] John Paul II notes that, while the widening of access to public work is in some senses a genuine gain, it is not without loss. Throughout John Paul II's writings, as in his Apostolic Letter *Mulieris Dignitatem* and his *Letter to Families*, he points out that men and women arrive at their true stature only through self-donating love. In women this gift of self is realized distinctively through the nurturing of a child. Thus, motherhood in women (which can be expressed also in the nurture of spiritual children) needs to be honored even above the valuable contributions that women make in the political and economic spheres.[167] Sadly, today the mater-

---

[165] Believers may look to the prophet Elijah, the book of the Psalms, our Lord, and, of course, the Virgin Mary as exemplars of prayer, which, as we learn from St. John Damascene is "the raising of one's mind and heart to God" (De fide orth., 3, 24; CCC 2559). The *Catechism* helpfully distinguishes between six kinds: blessing, adoration, petition, intercession, thanksgiving, and praise (CCC 2643–2644).

[166] On the impact of John Paul II's thought see, for instance, Leonie Caldecott's chapter, "Sincere Gift: The New Feminism of John Paul II," in *John Paul the Great: Maker of the Postconciliar Church*, ed. William Oddie (San Francisco: Ignatius Press, 2005), 109–129.

[167] "Parenthood—even though it belongs to both—is realized much more fully in the women, especially in the pre-natal period. It is the women who 'pays' directly for this shared

nal role has been so derided that many find it neither desirable nor possible to nurture the family at home. A society in which government makes it easy to divorce and hard for moms to stay home is not progressive, but dying. To this end John Paul II argued that "society must be structured in such a way that wives and mothers are *not in practice compelled* to work outside the home" (FC 23). This is not an unrealistic hope. Laws could stop penalizing women who stay at home. As a start: greater federal and local tax relief could be redirected toward families with dependent children; zoning laws could allow for the greater use of the home as a place of work; homeschooling families might be relieved from some portion of property taxes; and so forth.[168] Most important, women and their husbands will have to rediscover the beauty of motherhood.

Catholics will have to reevaluate the concept of equality, beginning with its unit of measurement. Obviously, neither a reduction in men's height nor an increase in women's weight is in view. Equality is measured usually by a vote, by a wage, by a raise — in other words, according to some political or economic criterion. Even accepting for the moment a strictly materialist

---

generation, which literally absorbs the energies of her body and soul. It is therefore necessary that the man be fully aware that in their shared parenthood he owes a special debt to the woman. No programme of 'equal rights' between women and men is valid unless this fact is fully taken into account" (*Mulieris Dignitatem*, 18).

[168] For reflections on an economy responsive to the needs of the family see Wendell Berry's *Home Economics: Fourteen Essays* (New York: North Point Press, 1987) and Allan Carlson's "Beyond Capitalism and Socialism: Rebuilding the American Economy Focused on Family and Community," in *The Chesterton Review* (Spring/Summer 2010): 101–112.

conception of equality, it is a long time since we have passed from equality of opportunity to the practical necessity of conformity. Moving beyond Marx, happiness, for Catholics, is not measured chiefly by dollars and cents. Virtue is a far more stable currency. Is it really the case that most women are happier at the office rather than in the home? Given the toxic results of social engineering now evident, there is some prima facie evidence that the pursuit of abstract equality so defined works against the happiness of both sexes and our children. It is notable that women consistently say that they do not derive their greatest satisfaction from work outside the home. This preference is all the more marked for women with children. In a recent study, when mothers with children under eighteen were asked about their most important source of fulfillment, 51 percent cited their relationship with their children, 29 percent cited their relationship with their husband or common-law husband, and only 1 percent cited their job or career. [169] Why is it expected that women cannot be fulfilled in the home? Marriage and teen catechesis in this area should move to the offensive.

Recently, a couple we know sought advice from their Anglican priest on whether they should try to conceive a third child. The pastor encouraged them to do so; he explained that he had counseled many parents who regretted not having had more children, but he had never met a couple who thought they had raised too many. Fewer couples are willing to pursue this path, however, when both parents pursue a full-time career into their thirties. Children are a blessing; welcoming them does require

---

[169] Additionally, nine out of ten said that their marriage makes them happy all or most of the time (Pew Research Center, "Motherhood Today—A Tougher Job, Less Ably Done," May 1997, www.people-press.org).

that we adjust our spending habits. If we really think that raising children is a nobler task than accumulating wealth, then it may be that young married couples will have to lower their economic expectations. In short, Catholics will need to relearn to make the case not only for traditional marriage but also for openness to many children, for human flourishing requires love as well as a sound economy and stable polity. And there is no better way to learn how to love than in a family that is open to life.

Large families can foster holiness for a variety of reasons. For the parents, here are three: less sleep, higher costs, and more work — three great reasons, some might say, for willfully *avoiding* children altogether. And many do. But not if your aim is Heaven. Indeed, the fruits of conjugal love produce the conditions by nature that monks and nuns have to impose upon themselves by grace (i.e., by accepting the evangelical counsels of poverty, chastity, and obedience).

Along these lines there is a famous story from St. Thérèse of Lisieux's life at Carmel. Then as now, within a monastery a bell is the common call to prayer. So prompt was Thérèse's obedience that at its first ring she would throw down her pen, leaving behind a half-formed word on the page. Well, in the domestic church, the cry of a child is like St. Thérèse's bell; it often tolls.

No doubt, it does not always work for a mother to stay at home. Nor are all couples open to life blessed with children. These absences are a cause of sorrow to such parents. Sadly, more and more couples see gain in what past times have recognized as a loss. In virtually every human culture large families have been a sign of blessing. According to the *Catechism* they still are: "Sacred Scripture and the Church's traditional practice see in large families a sign of God's blessing and the parents' generosity" (CCC 2373). Children bless grandparents and cousins because they carry infectious joy; children bless brothers and sisters because they offer immediate friendship; children bless Mom and Dad, above all, because they turn parents into adults. Unlike any other gift, a new baby offers parents the opportunity to grow in love. The exchange of such gifts is possible only when a man and woman open themselves up to new life. The Church continues to esteem those who do so without reserve.

Conclusion

In concentrating on the family we have concerned ourselves not so much with the fruits of Christian prayer as with its roots. In the usual course of a believer's life, the habits of prayer are established first in childhood, in the native soil of the family. Since the birth of Marxism in the mid-nineteenth century until about 1980, it was almost universally assumed that social-scientific research was the friend of left-leaning social engineers. Early on the social sciences adopted Marx's assumption that social relations not characterized by strict material equality are unjust. Statistical and empirical research were welcomed as a means of uprooting the prejudice and irrationality upon which traditional institutions were founded. Above all—the argument went—the family, and with it the roles of men and women, would be exposed as having no hold in nature. All this has changed. Many sociologists remain wedded to radical politics. But their grip on the discipline has loosened. For many years now, social-scientific studies relating to the family have helped to illuminate "the strengths, indeed the irreplaceability of the family."[170] In response to Engels, de Beauvoir, MTV, and

---

[170] So conclude Allan Carlson and William L. Saunders, Jr., in the preface to *A Portrait of the Family*, ix. In affirming the value of social-scientific research I do not suppose its independence

company, catechesis will have to harness more confidently the abundant research available on the benefits of family. As reason and revelation attest, a communion of persons is founded not upon abstract equality but upon a willingness to serve Christ in one another. In the renewal of Catholic culture, the battle begins at home, on bended knee.

from philosophy or theology. Theology always retains its own authority to judge the moral implications drawn from statistical and empirical research. As John Paul II writes: "The Church values sociological and statistical research, when it proves helpful in understanding the historical context in which pastoral action has to be developed and when it leads to a better understanding of the truth. Such research alone, however, is not to be considered in itself an expression of the sense of faith" (FC 5). On the place of social-statistical research in Catholic research on marriage see Mary Shivanandan, *Crossing the Threshold of Love: A New Vision of Marriage in the Light of John Paul II's Anthropology* (Washington, DC: Catholic University of America Press, 1999), 209–270.

Christ Risen from the Tomb, Bergognone, Italian, c. 1490, tempera on panel

8

On Prayer:
What Christ Pleads

From the lex orandi *to the* lex credendi

At the high point of Antonio's trial in the *Merchant of Venice*, Portia asks for clemency before an exacting Shylock, who will not be satisfied with less than a pound of Antonio's flesh on collateral for his loan. In Portia's famous encomium on mercy Shakespeare offers this insight into the function of prayer.

> But mercy is above this sceptred sway,
> It is enthroned in the hearts of kings,
> It is an attribute to God himself;
> And earthly power doth then show likest God's
> When mercy seasons justice. Therefore, Jew,
> Though justice be thy plea, consider this,
> That in the course of justice, none of us
> Should see salvation. We do pray for mercy,
> And that same prayer doth teach us all to render the
> The deeds of mercy.
>
> (Act 4, scene 1)

Prayer teaches us the value, and so the limits, of earthly justice. Portia's words illustrate the movement within Christian culture from the *lex orandi* to the *lex credendi*, from the law of prayer to the law of belief. The final section of the *Catechism* is a meditation upon the prayer of Jesus. As Christ unveiled the pattern of Christian discipleship in the Sermon on the Mount, so he modeled for us the way of prayer in his seven petitions. And, there is no prayer that teaches better than the Our Father. Tertullian described it as "the summary of the whole gospel" (*De orat.*, 1; CCC 2761); St. Augustine concluded, "I do not think that you will find anything in [Scripture] that is not contained and included in the Lord's Prayer" (*Ep.*, 130, 22; CCC 2762).

Of the seven petitions of Christ I wish to highlight only the second: "Thy Kingdom come." According to the *Catechism* these words refer "primarily to the final coming of the reign of God through Christ's return" (CCC 2818). Above all Jesus' words teach us to hope for eternal life. In our final meditation we consider: How does this hope for Heaven transform the character of our discipleship on earth?

As I wish to show, these final pages of the *Catechism* draw us into the heart of our enquiry into the relationship between faith and culture. Prayer shapes our aspirations. It teaches us what to place our hope in. That is the positive lesson. Christ's plea clarifies what kind of success the gospel may and may not be expected to yield in the present age. In other words, if we are to learn from Christ's prayer we will also have to unlearn a great deal. At the origin of the modern era was a rejection of the Christian hope of eternal life in favor of a worldly salvation, a turn from eschatology to utopia. This turn away from an otherworldly expectation has undermined Catholic culture of recent years. The last chapter argued that the seeds of mysticism most naturally germinate in the soil of the domestic church. Here we shall point out how the fruits of Christian mysticism require that some set aside even intrinsic goods, such as wealth and family. The Church looks first not to philosophers, nor to artists, nor to politicians, nor even to families, but to monks, nuns, and sisters to bear witness to the ultimate object of our hope.

As it turns out, the best way to live in the world is to realize that we are created for another world; just as, conversely, the surest way to destroy the earth is to pretend that there is no Heaven. Our first task will be to show how it is that the virtue of hope was twisted in the service of a secularized eschatology in the modern era. After that, we will show why the renewal of culture depends so heavily upon men and women who have abandoned the world out of love.

From eschatology to utopia

The second of Pope Benedict XVI's trio of encyclicals on the virtues is on Christian hope. Distilling a long career of reflection upon the theological differences between Christian eschatology and secular utopia, *Spe Salvi* offers a helpful framework for identifying the nature of the transformation of hope in the modern era.[171]

At the origin of the modern turn, Benedict points to a new correlation between science and praxis. For the ancients philosophy was first of all the *contemplation* of nature; nature provided a norm for action. By contemplation we discover an order of the cosmos that teaches us also about ourselves. The turning of the seasons, the motions of the heavens, and nature's abundance are all thus read as signs of God's provision. As nature speaks to us of intentions and is a norm for judgment, so right

---

[171] For background see J. Christopher Paskewich, "Liberalism Ex Nihilo: Joseph Ratzinger on Modern Secular Politics," in *Politics* 28, issue 3 (2008): 169–176.

judgment about the use of freedom is the fruit of its contemplation. But like the letters on a page, nature's book also has to be interpreted. In the essay "Reflections on the Right Use of School Studies with a View to the Love of God" Simone Weil expressed well this classical approach to nature:

> Attention consists of suspending our thought, leaving it detached, empty, and ready to be penetrated by the object; it means holding in our minds, within reach of this thought, but on a lower level and not in contact with it, the diverse knowledge we have acquired which we are forced to make use of.... Above all our thought should be empty, waiting, not seeking anything, but ready to receive in its naked truth the object that is to penetrate it.[172]

Of course there were differences between the classical and patristic accounts of how nature ought to be studied. But it was a case of extension rather than of revision. Biblical revelation added to Greek philosophy; revelation explained why nature (i.e., fallen nature) can communicate beauty, order, justice, and at the same time disorder. Nature had suffered loss but would yet be transformed by grace. Christ's Resurrection was the firstfruits of the redemption of nature and the cosmos; his victory over death was a proof and an example of what lay ahead. These are all significant gains over the classical view. But whereas Christianity developed the classical view of nature, modernity made a sharp break with both.

For Francis Bacon (1561–1626) nature is no longer a norm; she is a lady ripe for conquest. With this new view of nature the

---

[172] In *Waiting for God*, 111–112.

aim of philosophy is turned on its head, from contemplation to action. Marx's dictum makes explicit the modern way of thinking: "Philosophers have hitherto only interpreted the world in various ways; the point is to change it."[173] Of course, the shift had occurred long before. What the experimental method of scientific observation affords, in Bacon's view, is the interpretation of nature *insofar as this can allow for its manipulation*. What is altered is the *aim* of science. Most scientists no longer read nature as we would a book, where we trust that the words on the page express the wish of its author. It is not a case where teleology was shown to be false; it is rather that scientists stopped being interested. Now, instead of turning to nature as a student or a lover, with a posture first of receptivity and wonder, armed with technique, man approaches with a whip. Man extends his power over nature, but ironically becomes less acquainted with her ways. In Bacon's words, the increase in knowledge of nature's laws yields "the triumph of art over nature" (*victoria cursus artis super natura*) (*Novum Organum*, 1.117; SS 16). In any event, the theological implications of the new approach were not lost on Bacon. The science of the future, Bacon hoped, would return our dominion over the natural environment. Science would lead us partway back into the Garden of Eden:

> For man by the fall fell at the same time from his state of innocency and from his dominion over creation. Both of these losses however can even in this life be in some part repaired; the former by religion and faith, the latter by arts and sciences.[174]

[173] This is taken from Marx's *Theses on Feurerbach* (thesis 11).

[174] Francis Bacon, *Novum Organum*, II.52 , ed. Fulton H. Anderson (New York: Liberal Arts Press, 1960), 267; for a general

Bacon's turn to the empirical method was a decisive first step in the long road we have traveled away from the Christian concept of hope.[175] Desire for Heaven was replaced by hope for a heavenly earth. Pope Benedict has observed that what has changed for those who accept this view is precisely the meaning of *redemption*:

> Anyone who reads and reflects on these statements attentively will recognize that a disturbing step has been taken: up to [Bacon's] time, the recovery of what man had lost through the expulsion from Paradise was expected from faith in Jesus Christ: herein lay "redemption." Now this "redemption," the restoration of the lost "Paradise" is no longer expected from faith, but from the newly discovered link between science and praxis. (SS 17)

In Benedict's analysis, one way of describing the genesis of modernity is the self-consciousness of man's capacity to shape *history*, the acceptance of a new correlation between science

---

orientation to Bacon's view of the relation between science and religion see J.C. Briggs, "Bacon's Science and Religion," in *The Cambridge Companion to Bacon*, ed. M. Pertonen (Cambridge: Cambridge University Press, 1996), 172–200, especially 176–177 and 192–197.

[175] Bacon's turn from the contemplation of nature to its mastery was not isolated. What Bacon instigated in natural philosophy, Machiavelli (1469–1527) had instigated in political science. Machiavelli did not see perfected nature as a norm but called for a new science of human society that would take its lead not from ideal, i.e., perfect justice, but from the workings of justice in our fallen condition. On this see further *The Prince*, trans. Harvey C. Mansfield, 2nd edition (Chicago: University of Chicago Press, 1998), 61.

and activity. History becomes the site for the gradual expansion of freedom. Expansion is made possible not by God's activity but through scientific mastery, through technology. Hope no longer anticipates eternal life. Hope looks instead to an increase of material and moral progress in this world. The very concept of the kingdom of God is made immanent.[176] In short, through the turn from eschatology to utopia, faith in God becomes faith in progress as such: material and moral progress on earth.

Pope Benedict identifies two problems with the secular view of hope: (1) political structures never adequately answer our desire for justice; as a consequence (2) worldly goods are not stable enough to justify confidence in the future.

First, political programs have inherent limitations. Clearly, government serves an essential good. Its primary task is to ensure law and order; but when government attempts to do more, it achieves less. Political structures are inadequate because, in order to be just, they cannot control everything. Nor should they try. Excessive intervention can thwart initiative and destroy freedom. A small business, a soccer club, a religious community, and a family each have their own ways of organizing

[176] From these origins in the sixteenth century we can trace also the transformation of hope into more recent times. Both Kant and Marx saw revolution as a means for making practical this new understanding of science and praxis. Kant, whose work anticipates and reflects upon the results of the French Revolution of 1789, looked forward to a utopia founded upon rational politics. As biblical—and hence ecclesiastically defined—faith receded, he hoped that it would be replaced by faith based upon reason alone. Its advance he described in these terms: "The gradual transition of ecclesiastical faith to the exclusive sovereignty of pure religious faith [i.e., faith based on reason alone] is the coming of the Kingdom of God" (quoted in SS 19).

relationships among members. As Alexis Tocqueville observed in his seminal work *Democracy in America* (1835), healthy republics depend upon intermediary communities to educate citizens in virtue. Between the state and the individual lie multiple regulating structures, such as guilds, the Church, and the family.[177] Each must be given its due. In Catholic social teaching, this insight is contained within the principle of subsidiarity, which can be stated as follows: "A community of a higher order should not interfere in the internal life of a community of a lower order" (CCC 1883). Thus, while law can and must encourage virtue, it must also allow for personal initiative, and make some room even for the misuse of freedom. If a political system could somehow guarantee peace, let us say, through the manipulation of mass media, through drugs, through governmental agents, or any other such techniques described in Aldous Huxley's *Brave New World*—we should not thereby have secured justice, since man's freedom would be denied. To welcome such a system would only have been to welcome the rule of the Antichrist.

To those who look to political and economic structures as the source of human salvation, Pope Benedict offers this caution:

> Freedom must constantly be won over for the cause of good. Free assent to the good never exists simply by itself. If there were structures which could irrevocably

[177] Mary Ann Glendon uses Tocqueville's observations as the starting point for her reflections in "The Cultural Underpinnings of America's Democratic Experiment," in *Building a Healthy Culture: Strategies for an American Renaissance*, ed. Dom Eberly (Grand Rapids, Michigan: Eerdmans Publishing Co., 2001), 41-58.

guarantee a determined—good—state of the world, man's freedom would be denied, and hence they would not be good structures at all. (SS 24)

Goods of this world are not enough. Men and women desire more than what can be transported across smooth roads that are paid for by fair taxes. Created in God's image we are satisfied only by an unconditional *love*. It is not merely that we seek affection. We require a redeeming love, a love strong enough to heal our minds and gracious enough to render us lovable. Christian hope is not a matter of optimism; it is not the expectation of steady progress through democracy and science; it is the anticipation of everlasting life with God, his angels, and all his saints. Only such an unchanging good could serve as the foundation for hope. Natural man thus finds his desire frustrated. He longs for some secure basis for hope; but temporal goods and earthly justice will not suffice. Our dilemma: live without hope in this world or learn to look elsewhere.

Prayer as a school of hope

To pray, "Thy kingdom come" is to set our hope upon a good that is present yet unseen. It is to discover the one good that is capable of answering to our longings for peace, of sustaining our efforts for justice, of justifying our hope in final victory. At this point some will object. Does not the hope of Heaven unravel our sense of responsibility on earth? Many believe so. A relief agency recently ran an advertisement with a clever slogan: *We believe in life before death.* We are realists, the organization meant to say; we care for the present. Of course, care for the body is noble. Yet the implied disjunction between body and soul is misguided.

Annunciation, Jan van Eyck, Netherlandish, c. 1434, oil on canvas

We can go a step further. Far from hampering our efforts in the world, the virtue of hope renders our service more effective. For one thing, keeping in view the kingdom of God gives us a fixed standard. Progress is good, but it is a good always measured in relation to some unit. It is not clear where on earth we could find an all-sufficient unit. As the bitter political experiments of the twentieth century have made plain, from the gas chamber to the Gulag, godless politics are inhuman politics. A purely secular society is unfit for human habitation. Progress needs to be gauged by something more than the GDP. Man is a *homo religiosus* (cf. CCC 28). He cannot help but render worship. Proclaim nothing as sacred, and you will find him scratching in the dirt in search of idols. Keeping in sight the kingdom of Heaven saves politics and man from degradation.

It saves us also from taking shortcuts. Just consider the proposals now endorsed by bioengineers and the pharmaceutical companies that back them. We are constantly encouraged to sacrifice the lives of a few for the liberation of many. Celebrities make their appeals in front of cameras; politicians assure us that "the science is settled"; progress marches on. Indeed, what man in his right mind would stand in the way of a cure for any disease? Yet, opposition persists. The reason is rarely because of an aversion to science. Conservative and religious opposition to certain bioethical developments, as Leon Kass, Chairman of the United States President's Council on Bioethics from 2001–2005 has ably explained, stems not from intransigence but from the stubborn belief that not every decision should be reduced to a cost-benefit analysis.[178] Or to say it another way: some costs are never worth incurring. Religious believers have an added sanction against the taking of innocent life; as St. Paul put it, "It is not licit to do evil that good may come of it" (Rom. 3:8). Realism is a virtue only to the extent that it takes into account all that belongs to reality, including the reality of the moral

---

[178] On this see, for instance, *Beyond Therapy: Biotechnology and the Pursuit of Happiness*, A Report of the President's Council on Bioethics (New York: Dana Press, 2003); under the leadership of Kass, the council also produced a textbook of readings: *Being Human: Readings from the President's Council on Bioethics* (New York: W. W. Norton, 2004).

law and our dignity as persons. In an age in which enlightened opinion generally favors abortion, euthanasia, and the cloning of body parts, it turns out that believing in life after death supplies one of the sturdier defenses for the conviction that there should be life before death, too.

Christian hope quickens our work in one final way. In addition to providing an objective measure of good and evil, it offers a subjective motive for action. Even when good plans fail, hope in final conquest continues to inspire. Hope based on eternal life preserves us from frantic toil as much as from paralyzing despair. Here we require a distinction. Being saved from despair is not to be shielded from sorrow. Even the one closest to Jesus on earth and in Heaven is known, at least by one of her titles, as Our Lady of the Seven Sorrows. Hope in God will not somehow purchase for the believer a backstage pass that spares him from having to live through the horrors of the show. The Church prays in the great Marian hymn at the close of the day, "To you do we send up our sighs, mourning, and weeping in this valley of tears." Christian hope is not therefore to be confused with optimism. Optimism is the detritus left on the mud after the tide of Christian faith has retreated. What has been left is about as useful for sailing as a pile of polished stones: it retains the smell of the sea, but none of its vital motion. So also the secular parody to hope, optimism is really only the baseless wish that in spite of the abyss all will be well.

No one escapes the valley without suffering. Countless examples from the lives of the saints could illustrate this principle. Here is one from living memory. In 2007 Mother Teresa's private diaries were published in English for the first time under the title *Come Be My Light*. Among other things this collection offered a glimpse into the agonizing self-doubt she suffered during her years in Calcutta. She confesses openly to the great "contradiction" in her heart. At times her love is strong; at other moments, "Souls hold no attraction—Heaven means nothing—to me it looks like an empty place." She confesses that her smile "is a big cloak" that actually "covers a multitude of pains."[179] When these and other revelations about her struggle were released, some in the secular press rejoiced. Triumph sounded for some as though what had come into their hands was a long-awaited vindication of all those philosophy and psychology classes they attended: Hurray! We are only beasts after all! Here was poor Mother Teresa at last exposed. The celebrity saint who seemed to defy the philosophy of egoism was found out to be just like one of us, but worse: she was *only pretending* to be good.

Come Be My Light gives vivid testimony to Christian suffering. In a note written for her confessor she admitted to a profound absence, as in this excerpt.

> In my heart there is no faith—no love—no trust—there is so much pain—the pain of longing, the pain of not being wanted.—I want God with all the powers of my soul—and yet there is terrible separation.[180]

Most of us do not even show up among the truly destitute. Mother Teresa never left. For all this suffering, all this doubt, all this lack of intimacy, the woman remained devoted to the God she could not feel. After one of the retreats that she attended by Fr. Picachy—her confessor and a friend of the

[179] Mother Teresa, *Come Be My Light: The Private Writings of the Saint of Calcutta*, edited with commentary by B. Kolodieschuk (New York: Doubleday, 2007), 169, 176.
[180] Ibid., 193.

community—Mother Teresa recorded the gift of consolation she had received. She thanked Fr. Picachy:

> The only way I have to show you my gratitude is by offering everything in me for your intentions. The darkness—the loneliness and pain—the loss and the emptiness—of faith—love—trust—these are all I have and in simplicity I offer them to God for your intention as a token of gratitude.[181]

Is hope in a future kingdom justified? If it is not, then such a woman is to be pitied. If there be no kingdom beyond earth, then each one who sacrifices his comfort, his past, his future, and his respectability for the gospel is proven a fool. Hope is reasonable only if that future reality can make itself known in some fashion. The Sisters of Charity are kind; but they are not foremost a charitable organization. Their witness demonstrates how prayer transforms, how prayer is a school of hope, and how its exercise draws the future into the present.

The consecrated life and Catholic renewal

St. Paul reminded the Corinthians, "There are a variety of gifts, but the same Spirit" (1 Cor. 12:4). Among the vocations within the Church is the consecrated life. Its relevance to the renewal of Catholic culture can perhaps best be seen against the background of the general map to holiness that all must follow. So we turn next to the map and then to one specific territory.

There are many paths to holiness; there are also definable stages along the journey. The doctrine of the degrees of illumination is present already in the Gospels. Christ, for example,

---

[181] Mother Teresa, *Come Be My Light*, 186.

Melk Abbey, Melk, Austria

spoke to the crowds only in parables. To his disciples, to those to whom it had been given "to know the secrets of the kingdom," he spoke openly (Matt. 13:10). St. Paul likewise distinguished between the unspiritual and the spiritual believer (1 Cor. 2:14). The fathers of the Church carried forward this habit. Conversion is an unfolding event. God initiates from the outside, but never without requiring that we be transformed within. All the fathers ancient and modern are united in this teaching. St. Gregory of Nyssa spoke of levels of ascent of the soul, as did St. Augustine, St. Bonaventure, and St. John of the Cross.[182] Amid the many levels or gradations of maturity long custom has isolated three phases: the purgative way, the

[182] See the whole of Gregory of Nyssa's *De vita Moysis*, Augustine's *De quantitate animae* §33, and Bonaventure's *Itinerarium mentis in Deum*, prol. §3; see also Reginald Garrigou-Lagrange, *The Three Ages of the Interior Life: Prelude of Eternal Life*, trans.

illuminative way, and the unitive way. Under the heading of "Whether charity is rightly distinguished into three degrees" St. Thomas answers in the affirmative and describes each:

> In like manner the diverse degrees of charity are distinguished according to the different pursuits to which man is brought by the increase of charity. For at first it is incumbent on man to occupy himself chiefly with avoiding sin and resisting his concupiscences, which move him in opposition to charity: this concerns beginners, in whom charity has to be fed or fostered lest it be destroyed: in the second place man's chief pursuit is to aim at progress in good, and this is the pursuit of the proficient, whose chief aim is to strengthen their charity by adding to it: while man's third pursuit is to aim chiefly at union with and enjoyment of God: this belongs to the perfect who "desire to be dissolved and to be with Christ." (ST II-II, Q. 24, art. 9)

God can elevate a sinner as he chooses. More typically, however, and irrespective of the vocation to which you are called within the Church, progress in charity proceeds according to the sequence set out above. Stages of the spiritual life are like our growth from childhood to adolescence to maturity. Transitions can be traumatic. Movement from one level to another is sometimes likened to a passage through darkness.[183]

M. Timothea Doyle, OP (London: B. Herder Book Co., 1951), 1:230–38.

[183] St. John of the Cross, *Dark Night of the Soul* (1.8.2), trans. Kieran Kavanaugh, OCD, and Otilio Rodriguez, OCD, in *The Collected Works of Saint John of the Cross*, revised ed. (Washington, DC: Institute of Carmelite Studies Publications, 1991), 374.

These stages mark the common pattern of growth. Created in God's image and joined by common baptism, all believers share in the honor of serving the apostolic mission. As the *Catechism* puts it, among Catholics there exists "a true equality with regard to dignity" whereby "all cooperate in the building up of the Body of Christ" (CCC 872).

But some are called to witness in a special way to the Church's holiness. Common dignity does not efface all difference. There is a spiritual unity among believers, but the Catholic Church is a hierarchically constituted community made up of clergy, religious, and the lay faithful. Although all receive the call to holiness, not everyone is destined to reach this by identical means. As St. Paul says, "There are many gifts" (1 Cor. 12:4). And in the Church, consecrated religious carry in particular the ministry of *witness*. Quoting from the Second Vatican Council's Dogmatic Constitution on the Church, the *Catechism* states:

> For the People of God has here no lasting city ... [the religious life] reveals more clearly to all believers the heavenly goods which are already present in this age, witnessing to the new and eternal life which we have acquired through the redemptive work of Christ and preluding our future resurrection and the glory of the heavenly kingdom. (CCC 933; LG 44)

In brief, the religious life offers to the Church and to the world three goods: it witnesses to the future, reveals the glory of Heaven, and thereby renews our imagination on earth.

In light of these, and to close, I offer three distinctive contributions that religious can make to the renewal of Catholic culture.

First, religious life serves the renewal of culture by its *witness to the future*. By living apart from the world religious can teach us to see the world aright. Their discipline beckons those who become submerged under a mountain of details to recall what is the one needful thing, to hold tightly to the heavenly goods unseen, yet "present in this age." By their prayer, by fidelity to the counsels, even by their mode of dress, religious brothers and sisters serve as "a sign of the future age" (*futuri saeculi signum*) (CIC 607, no. 1). History has a goal, and religious help show us where it is headed. The monk's witness frees culture from the tyranny of history and gives us a glimpse of what is coming at its end.

In other words, historiography is at root a theological enterprise. Protestants hearken back to the past (some period prior to unjustified theological innovations), while contemporary neopagans anticipate the future (when religious "ideologies" will be transcended).

For the Church it is otherwise. Catholics long neither for the past nor for some endlessly deferred point on the horizon. History achieved its penultimate moment two thousand years ago. After the Holy Spirit descended at Pentecost, humanity awaits no such further revelation. Before history is the progression from stone tools to iron, from Assyrian rule to Roman; it is *salvation* history; it is the record of God's self-disclosure attested to first in Scripture but no less in Tradition. So for us, in this last hour the Bride awaits only the Groom's return.

It is not that the Church abjures new cures in medicine nor that Catholics must live like the Amish. As the Benedictine contribution to Western agriculture and scholarship makes plain, "those men in the history of the Church who have attended most to the things above have done most to transform things here below."[184] It is not that material progress is without value; it is simply that this or any other secular measure is relativized. In speechless eloquence the woman in her habit saves culture from the view that history has all but achieved its end (as communists used to say and some proponents of liberal capitalism still do), or equally, that history is without rhyme or reason (as the postmodernists claim). In witnessing to the future kingdom of God, religious free us from divinizing or despising the present.

Now let us take a step further. Second, and equally important, consecrated believers aid the renewal of culture by their *devotion to the divine majesty*. The monk seeks salvation by spending his life in the service of God's glory. As the council put it, religious make it "their chief aim to give themselves to God totally in perfect charity" (PC 11). Said differently, the monk offers his whole life in service "to the divine majesty" (PC 9). In praising God he saves his soul and sanctifies the world with it. By turning aside from the legitimate interests of family, money, and freedom, the monk models a more perfect obedience to the second petition of the prayer of Jesus.

How does this radical devotion serve the culture of the Church? In their worship of the divine majesty religious model the virtue of *disinterestedness*. Counter to the dominant technocratic, utilitarian, and hedonistic culture that drowns our humanity, the monk is a teacher of fruitful inefficiency. Religious can remind us how to love things for their own sake. On the value of this virtue in relation to our work Romano Guardini, a teacher of Pope Benedict XVI, explained that, although

---

[184] John Saward, *Sweet and Blessed Country: The Christian Hope for Heaven* (Oxford: Oxford University Press, 2005), 53.

economic interests deserve their due, these are not the most fundamental motives for work:

> When a man who is dominated by his interests works, then his work lacks precisely that which gives it value; that is, a sincere service to the thing itself. For him the first and chief consideration is how he can get ahead and further his career. He knows very little of the freedom of work and the joy of creation.... And yet disinterestedness is the only disposition which produces genuine work, the pure act, because it frees man for creativity. It alone gives rise to what is great and liberating, and only the man who works in this way gains interior riches.[185]

The principle of self-forgetting love applies equally to cult. While studying in England, for some years my family had the privilege of living down the road from an Oratorian house. During this time the community renovated the interior of the church building. As is fitting for a house of Catholic worship, no expense was spared. Would funds have been better directed elsewhere? Given the number of young vocations this house experiences, it would seem not. By enhancing the beauty of the house of God, this community of priests and brothers witness that there is no greater work than rendering glory to God.

There is a final dimension to this witness of religious. In pointing to the future, in serving the divine majesty, consecrated believers help *refresh the moral imaginations* of other Christians. From its beginnings in the third and fourth centuries, monastic life has been countercultural. The first monks escaped to the

---

[185] Romano Guardini, *Learning the Virtues That Lead You to God*, trans. S. Lange (Manchester, New Hampshire: Sophia Institute Press, 1992), 79–80.

desert because they feared the city. Such a fear was and is well founded. Nevertheless, the monk flees not because he is afraid of conflict. Just the opposite is the case. He takes flight to the literal desert of the country or to the figurative desert of his cell so as to enter into mortal combat. Monks and nuns, by seeking their own sanctification, take on the world—not the world that God created, for that is good, but the world insofar as it has become a principle of opposition to the good, as the King James Version memorably has it: "the lust of the flesh, and the lust of the eyes, and the pride of life" (1 John 2:15). By asceticism, through prayer, and in the ordering of his daily schedule, the religious models a way of life totally fixed upon Heaven. The lessons learned on this front can be applied by other Christians in other fields of battle who face the same war.

It is no coincidence that the decline in Catholic culture has occurred alongside the decline of religious life. Outsiders who did not live through the council often find inexplicable the convulsions among religious orders that followed. Seemingly overnight, religious went from singing the Divine Office to serving in soup kitchens to sitting in yoga classes.[186] The

---

[186] Often changes imposed upon women's religious orders were carried out against the express wishes of their members and by questionable means. See Ann Carey's *Sisters in Crisis: The Tragic Unraveling of Women's Religious Communities* (Huntington, Indiana: Our Sunday Visitor, 1997), 149–161. One elderly sister reflects that: "Most sisters, accustomed to obedience by long practice of their vow, and untrained in how to deal with the bulldozing methods of controlled (and at times dishonest) processes, suffer martyrdom in silence and in indescribable pain, at seeing their congregations being turned into entities to which they can in no way relate, at witnessing the destruction of the original values, charisms and traditions of their founders and foundresses" (p. 308).

Vatican Council document *Perfectae Caritatis*, which supposedly justified the ill-conceived reforms undertaken in many
congregations, was hardly revolutionary. It never suggested the
removal of religious habits, for instance. "The religious habit, as
a symbol of consecration, must be simple and modest, at once
poor and becoming" (PC 17). That was all.[187] Religious were
not asked to render themselves invisible; nor were they called
to become visible activists.[188] Unfortunately, in many congregations the call for renewal became an occasion for revolution.
Adaptation often meant silly imitation. Over a few short years
the lives of religious came to look far less otherworldly, the
impulse of obedience having been transferred from an ancient
rule to politically fashionable causes. As religious undressed
themselves, they became less attractive to new recruits. And
rightly so. What creature would voluntarily exchange a spouse
and a house full of children for old age in an apartment block?
Since 1965, the number of American religious sisters has fallen
from 179,000 to below 60,000. With the average age roughly
seventy years, the floor has not reached the bottom.

Still, all is not bleak. In recent years the Vatican has taken
an active interest in the problem and in 2009 launched an

---

[187] As one canon lawyer has remarked, "No sound interpretations
of conciliar and postconciliar legal texts even suggest that
wholesale abandonment of simple, identifiable garb for religious was (or is) intended" cited in Carey, *Sisters in Crisis*, 177.

[188] In the interest of renewing religious life allowance was made
for reforms, even for a measure of "prudent experimentation"
(PC 4). What principles were to guide this renewal? Renewal
comprises three things: a return to "the sources of the whole
Christian life" (*omnis vitae christianae fontes*), a return to
"the primitive inspiration" of the community, and their adaptation "to the changed conditions of our time" (PC 2).

On Prayer

Dominican Sisters of Mary Mother of the Eucharist,
Motherhouse Chapel, Ann Arbor, Michigan

investigation to find ways to help the Church help the sisters regain their confidence. On top of this, some orders are experiencing growth. To cite just a few examples, in the United States the Nashville-based Dominican Sisters of St. Cecilia have seen steady growth since about 1998; their community reports an average age of thirty-six. The more recent Dominican Sisters of Mary, Mother of the Eucharist, of Ann Arbor, Michigan, have an average age of twenty-six.[189]

Why are these orders growing? Young people interested in religious life are not looking for compromise. In 2009 a research center at Georgetown University attempted to identify two objects: the characteristics of those who join religious communities and features of the communities that attract. The report found the following:

[189] For statistics on these and other growing communities see the report by Ann Carey, "The CARA Study and Vocations," in *Catholic World Report* (May 2010): 14–17.

The most successful institutes in terms of attracting and retaining new members at this time are those that follow a more traditional style of religious life in which members live together in community and participate in daily Eucharist, pray the Divine Office, and engage in devotional practices together. They also wear a religious habit, work together in common apostolates, and are explicit about their fidelity to the Church and the teachings of the Magisterium. All of these characteristics are especially attractive to the young people who are entering religious life today.[190]

Here is a lesson applicable for all Christians, in every vocation in the Church. Be rigorous, be loyal, be proud of who you are. The radiance of the Bride is the most convincing proof of the love of the Bridegroom.

Lastly, by way of an addendum, although I have emphasized the particular and decisive contributions that religious make to the renewal of Catholic culture, it is not exclusively monks and nuns who can serve in these three ways. A multitude of communities invigorate the Church.

As an illustration of this, in 1947 Pope Pius XII formally recognized Secular Institutes as alternative models of discipleship. These are communities of consecrated persons who directly involve themselves in mission, service, or evangelization. While living in the world, members "strive for the perfection of charity" and seek to sanctify the world, "especially from within"

---

[190] From p. 117 of the study, "Recent Vocations to the Religious Life: A Report for the National Religious Vocation Conference," which was conducted by Georgetown's Center for Applied Research in the Apostolate, available on their website http://cara.georgetown.edu.

(CCC 928; quoting CIC 710).[191] Since the council, and with the encouragement of John Paul II, the Church has also witnessed an explosion of what are called new movements.[192] Consider the rapid growth of the Neocatechumenal Way, which operates in 900 dioceses in 105 countries and whose mandate is to promote catechesis. In 2006 members were granted a papal audience during which Pope Benedict XVI imparted his blessings upon the two hundred families associated with the movement who were being sent as missionaries throughout the world.[193] In 1982 John Paul II erected the first personal prelatures — institutions whose governance is linked not to territory but to persons. At present Opus Dei is the only such prelature. Its particular "pastoral or missionary work" (CIC 294) is to encourage holiness in daily life. Opus Dei is composed mostly of married people; only 2 percent of its 87,000 members are clergy.

The Church also recognizes Associations of the Christian Faithful, whose members "strive in common endeavor" to further apostolic works (CIC 298.1). One example is the Madonna House Apostolate, based in Combermere, Ontario. Founded in 1947 by Servant of God Catherine de Hueck Doherty and her

---

[191] There are some thirty secular institutes operating in the United States, including among them the Community of St. John and the Oblate Missionaries of Mary Immaculate.

[192] On this see Ian Ker, "The Radicalism of the Papacy: John Paul II and the New Ecclesial Movements," in *John Paul the Great: Maker of the Post-conciliar Church*, ed. William Oddie (San Francisco: Ignatius Press, 2005), 49–68, and Ratzinger's comments in *God and the World: A Conversation with Peter Seewald* (San Francisco: Ignatius Press, 2002), 454–456, which have not been contradicted during his pontificate.

[193] See the "Address of His Holiness Benedict XVI to Members of the Neocatechumenal Way Sending 200 Families for the Mission 'Ad Gentes,'" in *L'Osservatore Romano*, January 25, 2006.

husband, Eddie, its purpose is to embody the teachings of Jesus Christ "by forming a community of love." There are two hundred men, women, and priests in the community (in addition to associate clergy). Visitors report glowingly on the people, the heavy workload, the liturgy, the dormitory, and the setting. One striking feature of the community is their dining habits. Meals at Madonna House are modest—except on feast days. On holy days bright tablecloths, better fare, tinkling of glasses, and lusty singing make it clear to all that this day is set apart. And of course, a holy day should be a holiday.

Madonna House, Combermere, Ontario

The Great Red Dragon with the Woman Clothed with the Sun, William Blake,
British, c. 1805, pen and ink with watercolor

Conclusion

Catholic culture is shorthand for the way of life of a people. It is a way of life born of the Word of God and made visible in the lives of its hearers. Wherever the gospel encounters nations and tribes and tongues, what is human is taken up into what is divine and nevertheless not destroyed. Catholic culture is thus a culture informed by revelation, robed in flesh, enriched through time. Every front-yard nativity scene is the fruit of eight hundred years of tradition.

Since Cardinal Newman, and even more since the last council, the Church has become fully conscious of history. Doctrine builds upon the foundation of Scripture and the Fathers; but doctrine develops. So "as the centuries succeed one another," the Church moves "forward toward the fullness of divine truth" (DV 8). For the past forty years nobody has been allowed to forget this lesson, which is fine; the problem is that few teachers thought to remind us of what the doctrine of development implies for culture, which has brought disaster. Every development assumes a past stability, just as any leap into the air assumes that you first had two feet planted on the earth. This rule applies to the development of doctrine as surely as it does to the development of piety. Doctrines die without disciplines. Being bodily, we need truth to take form in color, texture, and smoke. What was missing after the council was an account and defense of the continuity of the embodied practices of the Faith that were to serve as the foundation for Christian renewal. Even a child can learn to call Mary *Theotokos*; but he is unlikely to think of her as his Mother until he has learned to thumb his way along a rosary.

The effects of this loss in transmission are now everywhere evident. The problem facing Catholics forty years ago was how sensibly to integrate the old with the new. The wrong answer was to attempt a revolution within the Church. Genuine gains of the council have been lost because much of the postconciliar generation "often has never experienced the devotional practices of previous generations" (DPP 59). The loss of the habit of piety coupled with the advance of an aggressive secularism has generated some predictable and some surprising results. What has been predictable is the way that young people, often after years of attendance in parochial schools, simply abandoned the Church. Once they leave home these cradle Catholics amuse themselves with the same coarse entertainments and excesses that their peers enjoyed with ease long before. Such baptized but unformed souls receive Communion at Christmas, ask for a Church wedding, and maybe even pray at the Requiem Mass of their grandmother; but they will never attend the fraternities, catechism classes, or processions that their parents took for granted. The sentimental among these will join the legion of "spiritual but not religious." They find their nourishment elsewhere, in yoga classes, or in a bowl of soft tofu.

The last fifteen years have also brought surprises. An alternative response to mushy religion has been the revival of orthodoxy. The cultural conditions that alienated some young people have galvanized others. These youth are the fruit of John Paul II's call for the New Evangelization and have been nothing but emboldened by the courage of Benedict XVI. Not only baby-boomer parents are bewildered; even veteran prelates express surprise at the intensity of these young Christians, some of whom are revitalizing traditional orders. For instance, in 2010, the American Dominican Province of St. Joseph took in their largest group of novices since 1966. Seeking to explain the causes of this renewal, Bishop Augustine Di Noia, OP, recently addressed the chapter of the province with comments that apply far beyond the northeastern United States:

> There is something afoot among the young men who are today being drawn to the priesthood and religious life, and thus to the Dominican Order.... My sense is that these 20 and 30 somethings have been radicalized by their experience before entering the Order in a way that we were not. I am not certain how they would articulate their experience for themselves. It is as if they had gone to the edge of an abyss and pulled back from it. Whereas we tended to experience modernity (and then post-modernity) as a kind of adventure that never or rarely touched the core of our faith, these 20 to 30 somethings have experienced the moral relativism and eclectic religiosity of the ambient culture—and possibly of their own personal experience—and recognized it as a chaotic but radical alternative to Christianity *with which no compromise is possible* [emphasis in original].[194]

[194] Most Rev. J. Augustine Di Noia, OP (at that time, June 2010), Secretary of the Congregation of Divine Worship and the Discipline of the Sacraments and Titular Bishop of Oregon City, "New Vocations in the Province of St. Joseph: Ecclesial, Historical and Cultural Perspectives" (Washington, DC: Dominican Vocation Office), 12–13.

Rebuilding Catholic Culture

Like Chesterton's Gabriel Syme in *The Man Who Was Thursday*, many young people today simply wake up to find themselves wishing to mount a "rebellion against rebellion," a revolt against anarchy, and they find that they discover freedom in the act. What undermines the freedom of the Church in the West is not Islam (or any other religion, for that matter), but secularism. As these young Catholics have well understood, like Christianity, secularism proposes itself as a universal culture. It apes religion but claims not to require faith. It is worth describing a few of the features of this rival culture.

Contemporary secularism's characteristics are seen most clearly against the backdrop of its origins in the Enlightenment. Between the seventeenth and the nineteenth centuries European intellectuals attempted to extract from Christianity moral principles that could win the allegiance of any rational person—any rational person, that is to say, alive to his own self-interest. When the Reformation shattered the spiritual and doctrinal unity of Europe, elements of Christendom survived, although in a mutated form. One of these was the old cosmopolitan outlook. From long exposure to the faith Europeans had come to see the unity of mankind as natural. You may have been born with yellow skin; you may have been educated inside Swiss borders; you may have married into the Kikuyu tribe; but such accidental predicates were secondary.

What really matters for Christians is that you are a child of God. In the twentieth century Europeans left God behind but hung on to the Kingdom. Protestants early on lost confidence in the unifying force of biblical religion and settled for Erastianism, state-controlled churches. For Roman Catholics, the inconclusive wars of religion and the compromise Treaty of Westphalia in 1648 dashed their hope for a unified Europe, at least for the foreseeable future. Both turned to foreign missions, while at home atheism advanced. Rather than stifle the drive for a universal culture, the success of France's revolution of 1789 only invigorated the effort to establish common norms, to extract the kernel of ethical rules from the husk of religious belief. After the thrashing, what remained? The grain of truth Enlightenment thinkers thought they discovered was the rights of *freedom*—of conscience, of scholarship, of elections, and most of all, of religion. Freedom would become in the modern world the one value against which every other good would be measured.

To understand the roots of modern secular humanism is therefore to appreciate how uniquely European a phenomenon it is. The scientific, rationalistic, and rights-based culture of modernity did not and could not have sprung out of any other soil than that which had been cultivated by fifteen centuries of the Faith. The concept of "inalienable human rights," for example, is as native to Islamic or indigenous Asian cultures as are blue jeans and Apple computers. They might find a home there; but they blew in from across the seas. Modern secularism is many things to many people, but it can have no meaning without first recognizing that it is a Christian heresy. It transgresses, it parodies, and thus presumes what it seeks to overcome.

The Second Vatican Council proclaimed rightly that the Church can share in the hopes and fears of the modern world. Yet as a philosophy and as a web of practices, the modern world has not unreasonably been called the "synthesis of all heresies."[195] Animating the modern project is the impulse to

---

[195] Pope Pius X once described modernism as an alternative system to orthodox Catholic teaching in his 1907 encyclical *Pascendi Dominici Gregis* (On the Doctrines of the Modernists), §39.

draw all people into a unified social order without dragging them through confessional disputes. From this motive has arisen the new moralism.

In setting God aside, the modern world did not stop trying to be good. In some ways it is too good. All the old Christian virtues of kindness and justice, of industry and thrift, were let loose on the world, but without any tether. Nobody knows what to do with them anymore, so they often crash into each other like the sounds of an orchestra without a score. The feminist may swear that truth is merely a white, middle-class, and phallocentric construct, but she will preach it to you with all the conviction of Elijah, oblivious to the irony of her passion. (If truth really is just an expression of one's own racial, sexual, or any other "interests," why should anyone else bother about hers—or his?) The environmentalist may preach a crusade against children, but if the earth should be saved, who will be left to enjoy it? When churchmen in the 1960s and 1970s proclaimed Catholicism's need to accommodate itself to the modern world, it was unclear what the Church needed to accommodate to, for this reason: the modern world is not one thing; it is only a very wild thing made up of component parts that have spun out of their natural orbits. [196]

As it turns out, the project of a universal culture based upon the extracted core of Christianity was doomed to fail. Christianity may indeed be an opiate, but to expect that sinners would behave like saints even after they were told that God is dead is willful delusion. Laws lose their force once citizens cease to regard their principles as based upon moral facts. There is a

[196] This is a theme admirably developed in Tracey Rowland's *Culture and the Thomist Tradition after Vatican II* (London: Routledge, 2003).

further problem. "Christian morals" without God cease to be Christian or moral. Severed from their roots in religion, ideals such as freedom, equality, and tolerance disappear like the morning mist under the hot sun of self-interest. This is one reason the persistent effort of some Catholics to prove themselves in solidarity with all things modern is wearisome. *Gaudium et Spes* rightly affirmed the nobility of dialogue. But dialogue requires the right setting. It assumes you are in for a duel, or at least a duet. When Catholics alienated themselves from their tradition, they vacated their own seat at the table. Sometimes with good faith, persons in leadership abdicated customary or legal privileges out of ill-conceived notions of fairness, ecumenism, or even humility. But neither skepticism nor ignorance promotes dialogue; they only cut it short. Enthusiasm for discussion without knowledge of and a firm loyalty to the Church's identity has led many Catholics to offer a sympathetic ear to almost any point of view except the Church's. Numerous schools and universities have been left as mere shells because their leaders twenty years ago stood up and wandered away. Over the next twenty years Catholics must sit down again and figure out how to start making up for past losses in the education of the young, for in the present culture wars, the conflict between believers and nonbelievers is precisely over the question of who or what defines what is reasonable.

This is not to say the Church cannot learn any lessons from modernity. Indeed, some impulses that have come out of the Enlightenment are recognized as universal by Christianity itself. We might mention the principle of religious freedom or the doctrine of human rights. Rightly formulated, these represent genuine gains that have been achieved by reason operating under the influence of and cooperation with secular philosophers.[197] But even here, at its strongest, secularism lacks. Consider the notion of religious freedom. Too often the separation of church and state in recent years has taken on a sinister turn. The distinction was a characteristically Christian innovation, seen neither in ancient Judaism, nor in classical Rome, nor in contemporary Islam. How, precisely, that division of authority ought to be settled in practice was often a bitter and bloody point of dissension (see the protracted controversies between the crown and the miter over the Church's right to invest bishops in medieval England). Be that as it may, once Christ denied the sword, once the Galilean told the crowd to render unto Caesar, political theory in the West was set on a novel trajectory. State and religion would not be unified again until the Reformation. And, as the history of modern totalitarian governments proves, life, liberty, and land are far more imperiled in atheistic states than in religious ones.

Religious freedom, then, is not a right to religious indifference. What it asserts is a limit upon the state's capacity to coerce belief. As the opening of the Second Vatican Council's *Dignitatis Humanae* has it, the doctrine of religious freedom "leaves intact the traditional Catholic teaching on the moral duty of individuals and societies toward the true religion and the one Church of Christ" (DH 1).[198] One need only consider the situ-

---

[197] On this see further Cardinal Ratzinger's "Subiaco Address," originally delivered at the Convent of Saint Scholastica, Subiaco, Italy, April 1, 2005, in *Christianity and the Crisis of Cultures*, trans. Brien McNeil (San Francisco: Ignatius Press, 2005), 34. The lecture also appears as an Appendix to Tracey Rowland's *Ratzinger's Faith*, 156–165.

[198] See the fine discussion by Fr. Regis Scanlon, OFM Cap., "Did Vatican II Reverse the Church's Teaching on Religious Liberty?" in *Homiletic and Pastoral Review* (January 2011): 61–68.

Conclusion

ation of Christians (and Muslims) living under Communism in 1964 or those in Pakistan or in Iran or in Saudi Arabia today, in order to appreciate the value of such an affirmation. At its best the doctrine aims to keep space open for God.

By contrast, in Europe and North America religious freedom increasingly means the exclusion of religion from the public. Rancor over prayer in school and nativity scenes on public land marks the sites of minor skirmishes. All the while, the slow erosion of religion from science, politics, the economy, and the family anticipates what the late Richard John Neuhaus called the making of the "naked public square." In such a context, appeal to revelation or tradition is out of the question. And, once reason itself is denied access to moral truth, even natural law is without force.

The rational character and hence public significance of faith is a matter upon which Catholics cannot yield. On many fronts what is needed is not more research but more nerve, and a longer memory. In the competition over which account of the universe is more rational, Christianity scores overwhelming advantages. Believers need to remember that it was the moderns, following Kant, who first threw down their arms. Secular-minded politicians and educators speak a great deal of "public reason," but reason in the modern world really has become a private matter.[199] In the modern view, reason does not bind us. Interests—in other words, our lower passions—are what unite. And who is to say that your passions are better than mine? When reason is only a tool, there is no one, except for

[199] On this see particularly Pope Benedict XVI's "Regensburg Address," reprinted in V.J. Schall, *The Regensburg Lecture* (South Bend, Indiana: St. Augustine's Press, 2007).

the Leviathan, who can say which desires are better or worse.[200] Force is all that can harmonize such interests.

But notice what else results. Once knowledge is reduced to what is replicable in the laboratory, the scientist can truly be said to rule. He is master. He reigns over a tiny kingdom, too small even to include himself. If the world really is nothing other than the product of chance, or if the stars spin merely by the motion of blind force, then the curtain falls. Freedom is illusory. The scientist whose brain is no more than the chemicals he studies not only ceases to rule; he stops being a person, as do other people, especially those who are materially beyond repair, or as yet unformed, in the womb. In a deterministic universe the researcher loses literally any reason to suppose that his thoughts, his discoveries, his conclusions—to say nothing of his dislikes and his loves—are of a quality different from any other blind interaction in the cosmos. Accept such premises and science, and along with it politics, no longer serves life but serves the rule of the mob.

We have perhaps devoted too much time to marking the dissolution of Catholic culture. What practical steps might we take toward its renewal?

I conclude with a strategy with four components. Let us end abortion; have more children; teach them Latin; and build better churches. These correspond, so it seems, to the most pressing social, educational, political, and liturgical needs of the Church in the West.

The first work of the physician is to stop the bleeding. Let us not be fooled by those who would reduce abortion to an evil

---

[200] See Frederick Vaughan's classic study, *The Tradition of Political Hedonism from Hobbes to J. S. Mill* (New York: Fordham University Press, 1982).

equivalent to unfair immigration rules. They are not equivalent. There are a thousand knotty problems today to which Catholics must offer reasoned judgments. Whether an innocent life should be defended is not among these. Neither war, nor the death penalty, nor open-pit mining are intrinsically evil acts, even though they might under certain conditions become evil. The only act of prudence that Catholics need to apply to the question of abortion is how to eliminate the practice. Justice toward children requires this victory. The social order depends upon it. Once the right to life is abrogated by government, no other secondary right is safe.

In addition to defending children, Catholics need to have more of them and to instruct them better. The irrationalists who presently dominate education would wipe away all record of the past. Teaching Latin is simply the most convenient way to instill memory and to begin to train a mind to think. In the present state of intellectual anarchy Catholic parents have to learn once again how to become midwives for their children, introducing them to what is noble and fine in the Catholic tradition of literature, history, and philosophy.

In the restoration of Catholic culture, there are many fronts on which to fight. But there is also a kind of order that should be respected. Culture follows cult. If Christian culture depends upon learning, it presupposes piety. Consequently, to tamper with liturgy is to alter our experience of God. And to alter our experience of God is to rearrange our view of his creatures. Thus activism and education—necessary as these are—will lose their way if not guided and nourished by a rich liturgical experience. Catholics have to remember how to build beautiful churches and learn again the habits of good manners once we step inside them. We might even say that the experience of ritual etiquette is the humus from which culture arises. Everyone from the most learned to the ignorant must plant their roots in this soil which, as Louis Bouyer once described it, is constituted "by the liturgical life in all its human and sacral fullness."[201] Given the often reckless experimentation of recent times, any rejuvenation of Catholic culture will depend upon a renewal of liturgical piety (a renewal now well underway). By stripping our worship of the dignity, the elegance, and the devotion that is its proper dress, too many pastors rendered it difficult for Catholics to understand, except in the most abstract terms, what it means to know the glory of the Lord.

The gospel is not only true; it is also beautiful. The recovery of beauty as a theological category has been one of the singular gains in Catholic thought in more recent reflection. As Pope Benedict XVI said recently to a gathering of some 260 artists at the Sistine Chapel, the apprehension of beauty is not external to our experience of God. "Authentic beauty," rather, "unlocks the yearning of the human heart, the profound desire to know, to love, to go towards the Other, to reach for the Beyond."[202] It will be for the younger generation of architects, painters, musicians, and writers to rediscover the Church's artistic patrimony, so as to translate such words into life-giving forms. We do not scorn scholarship. It is only that man cannot live on books alone.

But all programs for reform must be taken in the right spirit. Who knows under which fluorescent bulb the next great saint is studying or serving? In one very real sense there is nothing for us to *do*. As the Russian monastic Seraph of Serov (1759–1833)

---

[201] Louis Bouyer, *Decomposition of Catholicism*, 104.

[202] "Meeting with Artists: Address of His Holiness Benedict XVI," Sistine Chapel, November 21, 2009.

Conclusion

Christ Crucified between
Two Thieves, Schelte Boswart

memorably said, "Acquire a peaceful spirit and then thousands
of others round you will be saved."[203]

In sum, the fight for Catholic culture is a battle for the family, for the school, for the hospital, and for the Church. The
fragmentary condition of our age has left little middle ground
for those who would say neither yes nor no to Christ. Not only
does sanctity rely upon faith, so apparently does sanity. Though
we have largely left unexplored how Catholics might find common cause with other religious believers, this is not because

---

[203] As quoted in Kallistos Ware, *The Inner Kingdom* (Crestwood,
New York: St. Vladimir's Seminary Press, 2000), 133.

of a lack of possibilities. In this century Christians and theists of goodwill will find increasing friendship against a common Philistine. For, as St. Paul says, the Church can affirm "whatever is true" (Phil. 4:8) wherever it is found. This is only to be expected. Christianity is the religion of the "Logos." The world, for us, is born of the mind of God. Creation has come from reason, and will return to that same source. Unlike the secularist, believers thus have a way of accounting for beauty without retreating into sentimentality; of explaining morals without groveling before biology; of comprehending truth without denying the power of reason. Taken together, these advantages rise to a mountain of evidence that the generous heart longs to comprehend.

Him will I find: though when in vain
I search the feast and mart,
The fading flowers of liberty,
The painted masks of art.

I only find him at the last,
On one old hill where nod
Golgotha's ghastly trinity—
Three persons and one god.[204]

[204] G.K. Chesterton, "The Happy Man," in *The Collected Poems of G. K. Chesterton* (London: Cecil Palmer, 1929), 295.

Bibliography

Aquinas, St. Thomas. *Summa Theologica*. Translated by the Fathers of the English Dominican Province. 2nd ed. New York: Benzinger Brothers, 1948.

Aristotle. *Nichomachean Ethics*. Translated by T. Irwin. 2nd ed. Indianapolis, Indiana: Hackett Publishing Company, 1999).

Augustine, St. *On the Morals of the Catholic Church*. Translated by R. Stothert. In *Nicene and Post Nicene Fathers*, vol. 4. Peabody, Massachusetts: Hendrickson Publishers, 1995.

Balthasar, Hans Urs Von. *The Glory of the Lord, Vol. 5: The Realm of Metaphysics in the Modern Age*. San Francisco: Ignatius Press, 1991.

Baum, Gregory. *The Credibility of the Church Today: A Reply to Charles Davis*. London: Burns and Oats, 1968.

Bacon, Francis. *Novum Organum*, II.52. Edited by Fulton H. Anderson. New York: Liberal Arts Press, 1960.

Barrett, Justin L. *Why Would Anyone Believe in God?* Walnut Creek, California: Alta Mira, 2004.

Beauvoir, Simone de. *The Second Sex*. Translated and edited by H. M. Parshley. New York: Bantam Books, 1961.

Benedict XIV. "Address of His Holiness Benedict XVI to Members of the Neocatechumenal Way Sending 200 Families for the Mission 'Ad Gentes.'" In *L'Osservatore Romano*. January 25, 2006.

―――. "Meeting with Artists: Address of His Holiness Benedict XVI." November 21, 2009.

―――. "Service to the Human Family: Address to the UN General Assembly." In *Christ Our Hope: Homilies and Addresses in USA*. London: Catholic Truth Society, 2008.

Bess, Philip. *Till We Have Built Jerusalem: Architecture, Urbanism, and the Sacred*. Wilmington, Delaware: ISI Books, 2006.

Bibby, Reginald. "The Catholic Situation in North America: Magnificent Opportunities, Breathtaking Responsibility." In *Journal of Mission Studies* XIV (2007): 69–84.

―――. *Restless Gods: The Renaissance of Religion in Canada*. Toronto: Novalis, 2004.

Bloom, Allan. *The Closing of the American Mind*, New York: Basic Books, 1987.

Bolt, Robert. *A Man for All Seasons*. Toronto: Bellhaven House, 1974.

Bouyer, Louis. *The Decomposition of Catholicism*. Translated by C.U. Quinn Chicago: Franciscan Herald Press, 1969.

Briggs, J.C. "Bacon's Science and Religion." In *The Cambridge Companion to Bacon*. Edited by M. Pertonen. Cambridge: Cambridge University Press, 1996.

Bibliography

Burnet, John. *Essays and Addresses*. London: Chatto and Windus, 1929.

Caesar, M. *Dante: The Critical Heritage*. London: Routledge, 1999.

Caldecott, Leonie. "Sincere Gift: The New Feminism of John Paul II." In *John Paul the Great: Maker of the Post-conciliar Church*. Edited by William Oddie. San Francisco: Ignatius Press, 2005: 109–129.

Carpenter, H., ed. *The Letters of J.R.R. Tolkien*. London: Allen and Unwin, 1981.

Carey, Ann. *Sisters in Crisis: The Tragic Unraveling of Women's Religious Communities*. Huntington, Indiana: Our Sunday Visitor, 1997.

———. "The CARA Study and Vocations." In *Catholic World Report* (May 2010): 14–17.

Chesterton, G.K. *Orthodoxy*. San Francisco: Ignatius Press, 1995.

———. *The Collected Poems of G.K. Chesterton*. London: Cecil Palmer, 1929.

Clayton David. "The Way of Beauty." In *Second Spring: An International Journal of Faith and Culture* 4 (2003): 19–26.

Cross, S.H., and O.P. Sherbowitz-Wetzor, trans. and ed. *Russian Primary Chronicle*. Cambridge, Massachusetts: The Medieval Academy of America 1953.

Di Noia, Most Rev. J. Augustine. "New Vocations in the Province of St. Joseph: Ecclesial, Historical and Cultural

Perspectives." Washington, DC: Dominican Vocation Office.

Daniels, Cynthia R., ed. *Lost Fathers: The Politics of Fatherlessness in America*. New York: St. Martin's Griffin Press, 2000.

Dante. *Inferno*. Translated with notes by Dorothy Sayers. London: Penguin, 1949.

Day, Thomas. *Where Have You Gone, Michelangelo?: The Loss of Soul in Catholic Culture*. New York: Crossroads, 1993.

Derrida, Jacques. "Différance." In *Margins of Philosophy*. Translated with notes by Alan Bass. Chicago: University of Chicago Press, 1982.

Duggan, John, and Terry Fay, eds. *Spiritual Roots: Historical Essays on the Roman Catholic Archdiocese of Toronto at 150 Years of Age*. Toronto: Our Lady of Lourdes, 1991.

The Economist. "Gendercide: Killed, Aborted or Neglected, At Least 100 Million Girls Have Disappeared—and the Number Is Rising." March 6, 2010.

Eliot, T. S. *Notes Towards the Definition of Culture* in *Christianity and Culture*. New York: Harcourt, Brace and World, Inc., 1949.

———. *Selected Essays*. London: Faber and Faber, 1965.

Engels, Friedrich. *The Origin of the Family, Private Property, and the State*. New York: International Publishers, 1970.

Flanagan, Caitlin. "Why Marriage Matters." In *Time*, July 13, 2009: 45–49.

Bibliography

Garrigou-Lagrange, Reginald. *The Three Ages of the Interior Life.* 2 vols. Translated by Sr. M. Timothea Doyle. London: B. Herder Book Co., 1951.

Ginsberg, Warren. "Free Will." In the *Dante Encyclopedia.* Edited by Richard Lansing. New York: Garland Publishing, Inc., 2000, 425–427.

Grant, George. "Faith and the Multiversity." In *Technology and Justice.* Concord, Ontario: House of Anansi Press, 1986.

Gerrish, B. A. *Grace and Reason: A Study in the Theology of Luther.* Oxford: Clarendon Press, 1962.

Gilchrist, Michael. "New Improved English Mass Translation Nears Completion." In *AD 2000.* Vol. 17, no. 6 (July 2004): 3–4.

Glendon, Mary Ann, "The Cultural Underpinnings of America's Democratic Experiment." In *Building a Healthy Culture: Strategies for an American Renaissance.* Edited by Dom Eberly. Grand Rapids, Michigan: Eerdmans Publishing Co., 2001.

Guardini, Romano. *Learning the Virtues That Lead You to God.* Translated by S. Lange. Manchester, New Hampshire: Sophia Institute Press, 1998.

Irigaray, Luce. *This Sex Which Is Not One.* Translated by C. Porter. Ithaca, New York: Cornell University Press, 1985.

Jenkins, Philip. *The New Anti-Catholicism: The Last Acceptable Prejudice.* Oxford: Oxford University Press, 2003.

Kant, Immanuel. *Perpetual Peace*. In *Perpetual Peace and Other Essays*. Translated by T. Humphrey. Indianapolis, Indiana: Hackett Publishing, 1983.

Kelly, Michael. "The Wolves Roamed Freely: Recent Judicial Commission Reports Contain Devastating Findings about Abuse and Cover Up in the Irish Church." In *Catholic World Report* (February 2010): 28–30.

Ker, Ian. "The Radicalism of the Papacy: John Paul II and the New Ecclesial Movements." In *John Paul the Great: Maker of the Post-conciliar Church*. Edited by William Oddie. San Francisco: Ignatius Press, 2005.

Kolodieschuck, B., ed. *Come Be My Light: The Private Writings of the Saint of Calcutta*. New York: Doubleday, 2007.

Kreeft, Peter, and Fr. Ronald Tacelli. *Handbook of Catholic Apologetics*. San Francisco: Ignatius Press, 2009.

Levant, Ezra. *Shakedown: How Our Government Is Undermining Democracy in the Name of Human Rights*. Toronto: McClelland and Stewart, 2009.

Lubac, Henri de. *Medieval Exegesis, Volume 1: The Four Senses of Scripture*. Translated by M. Sebanc. Grand Rapids, Michigan: William B. Eerdmans, 1998.

———. *The Paradoxes of Faith*. San Francisco: Ignatius Press, 1987.

Lacordaire, Henri-Dominique. *Life: Conferences Delivered at Toulouse*. Translated by T. D. Langdon. New York: P. O'Shea Publishers, 1874.

Bibliography

Lewis, C. S. *The Magician's Nephew.* New York: Harper Trophy, 2000.

McNamara, Denis R. *Catholic Church Architecture and the Spirit of the Liturgy.* Chicago: Hillenbrand Books, 2009.

Maher, Bridget. *The Family Portrait: A Compilation of Data, Research and Public Opinion on the Family.* 2nd ed. Washington, DC: The Family Research Council, 2004.

Martinez, R., and R. Durling. *The Divine Comedy of Dante Alighieri: Vol 2: Purgatorio.* Oxford: Oxford University Press, 2003.

May, William E. "The Cultural and Ecclesial Situation 1964–1967: Paving the Way for Dissent from Church Teaching on Contraception." In *Fellowship of Catholic Scholars Quarterly* 32, no. 3 (Fall 2009): 10–19.

Messori, Vittorio. *The Ratzinger Report: An Exclusive Interview on the State of the Church with Joseph Cardinal Ratzinger.* Translated by S. Attanasio and G. Harrison. San Francisco: Ignatius Press, 1985.

Mommsen, Theodore. "Petrarch's Conception of the Dark Ages." *Speculum* 17, no. 2 (April 1942): 226–242.

Murray, Peter and Laura. *The Oxford Companion to Christian Art and Architecture.* Oxford: Oxford University Press, 1996.

National Education Office. *A Commitment to Higher Education in Canada: The Report of a Commission of Inquiry on Forty Catholic Colleges and Universities.* Ottawa, 1970.

Need, S. W. *Truly Human and Truly Divine: The Story of Christology and the Seven Ecumenical Councils*. Peabody, Massachusetts: Hendrickson Publishers, 2008.

Newman, John Henry Cardinal. *An Essay on the Development of Doctrine*. Foreword by Ian Ker. Notre Dame, Indiana: University of Notre Dame Press, 1989.

————. *Loss and Gain: The Story of a Convert*. London: Longmans, Green and Co., 1906.

Nichols, Aidan. *Christendom Awake: On Reenergizing the Church in Culture*. Grand Rapids, Michigan: William B. Eerdmans Publishing Co., 1999.

————. *The Shape of Catholic Theology: An Introduction to Its Sources, Principles, and History*. Collegeville, Minnesota: The Liturgical Press, 1991.

O'Donovan, Oliver. *The Desire of the Nations*. Cambridge: Cambridge University Press, 1997.

Paskewich, J. Christopher. "Liberalism Ex Nihilo: Joseph Ratzinger on Modern Secular Politics." In *Politics 28*, no. 3 (2008): 169–176.

Pattison, Robert. *The Triumph of Vulgarity: Rock Music in the Mirror of Romanticism*. Oxford: Oxford University Press, 1987.

Pearce, Joseph. *Tolkien: Man and Myth*. San Francisco: Ignatius Press, 1998.

Pevnser, Nikolaus. *An Outline of European Architecture*. 5th ed. London: Penguin, 1958.

Bibliography

Phillips, C., ed. *Gerard Manley Hopkins*. Oxford: Oxford University Press, 1990.

Ratzinger, Joseph Cardinal. *Principles of Catholic Theology: Building Stones for a Fundamental Theology*. Translated by Sr. M. F. McCarthy. San Francisco: Ignatius Press, 1987.

Ratzinger, Joseph Cardinal. *On the Way to Jesus Christ*. San Francisco: Ignatius Press, 2005.

————. "Subiaco Address." In *Christianity and the Crisis of Cultures*. Translated by Brien McNeil. San Francisco: Ignatius Press, 2005.

————. *God and the World: A Conversation with Peter Seewald*. San Francisco: Ignatius Press, 2002.

Richert, R. A., and J. L. Barrett. "Do You See What I See? Young Children's Assumptions about God's Perceptual Abilities." In *International Journal for the Psychology of Religion* 15, no. 4 (2005): 283–295.

Robinson, Jonathan. *The Mass and Modernity: Walking to Heaven Backward*. San Francisco: Ignatius Press, 2005.

Rousseau, Jean-Jacques. *Emile: Or, On Education*. Translated by Allan Bloom. New York: Basic Books 1979.

Rowland, Tracey. *Culture and the Thomist Tradition after Vatican II*. London: Routledge, 2003.

————. *Ratzinger's Faith: The Theology of Pope Benedict XVI*. Oxford: Oxford University Press, 2008.

Rosenberg, Harold. *The Tradition and the Now*. New York: Da Capo Press, 1996.

St. John of the Cross, *Dark Night of the Soul*. Translated by Kieran Kavanaugh, OCD, and Otilio Rodriguez, OCD, in *The Collected Works of Saint John of the Cross*. Rev. ed. Washington, DC: Institute of Carmelite Studies Publications, 1991.

Saward, John. *Sweet and Blessed Country: The Christian Hope for Heaven*. Oxford: Oxford University Press, 2005.

Schloeder, Steven J. *Architecture in Communion: Implementing the Second Vatican Council through Liturgy and Architecture*. San Francisco: Ignatius Press, 1998.

Schmemann, A. *For the Life of the World*. Crestwood, New York: St. Vladimir's Seminary Press, 1973.

Scruton, Roger. *Beauty*. Oxford: Oxford University Press, 2009.

————. *The Aesthetics of Architecture*. Princeton, New Jersey: Princeton University Press, 1979.

Shaidle, Kathy, and Pete Vere. *The Tyranny of Nice: How Canada Crushes Freedom in the Name of Tolerance and Why It Matters to Americans*. Toronto: Interim Publishing, 2008.

Shivanandan, Mary. *Crossing the Threshold of Love: A New Vision of Marriage in the Light of John Paul II's Anthropology*. Washington, DC: Catholic University of America Press, 1999.

Singleton, Charles. *Journey to Beatrice*. Baltimore: Johns Hopkins Press, 1958.

Smith, Janet E. *Humanae Vitae: A Generation Later*. Washington, DC: Catholic University Press of America, 1991.

Bibliography

Steyn, Mark. "True North Strong and Free." In *Macleans*, April 12, 2010.

Storkey, Elaine. *Origins of Difference*. Grand Rapids, Michigan: Baker Academic, 2001.

Stormon, E. J. ed. and trans. *Towards the Healing of Schism: The Sees of Rome and Constantinople*. Mahwah, New Jersey: Paulist Press, 1987.

Strauss, Leo. *What Is Political Philosophy? And Other Essays*. Chicago: University of Chicago Press, 1988.

Suger, Abbot. *On the Abbey Church of St.-Denis and Its Art Treasures*. Edited, translated, and annotated by Erwin Panofsky. 2nd ed. Princeton, New Jersey: Princeton University Press, 1979.

Sutton, Ian. *Western Architecture: A Survey from Ancient Greece to the Present*. London: Thames and Hudson, 1999.

Thérèse of Lisieux, St. *The Story of the Soul*. Translated by Ronald Knox. London: The Harvill Press, 1958.

Tolstoy, Leo. *Anna Karenina*. Translated by Constance Garnett. New York: The Bobbs-Merrill Co., 1978.

Topping, Ryan N. S. "Catholic Studies in Canada: History and Prospects." In *CCHA Historical Studies* 76 (2010): 45–60.

———. *St. Augustine*. London: Continuum, 2010.

Torgerson, Mark A. *An Architecture of Immanence: Architecture for Worship and Ministry Today*. Grand Rapids, Michigan: William B. Eerdmans, 2007.

Visser, Margaret. *St. Agnes Outside the Walls in Rome.* See her *The Geometry of Love: Space, Time, Mystery and Meaning in an Ordinary Church.* Toronto: HarperFlamingo, 2000.

Von Hildebrand, Alice. *By Love Refined.* Manchester, New Hampshire: Sophia Institute Press, 1989.

Waite, L. J. and M. Gallagher. *The Case for Marriage: Why Married People Are Happier, Healthier, and Better Off Financially.* New York: Doubleday, 2000.

Ware, Kallistos. *The Inner Kingdom.* Crestwood, New York: St. Vladimir's Seminary Press, 2000.

————. *The Orthodox Way.* Crestwood, New York: St. Vladimir's Seminary Press, 1990.

Weigel, George. *Witness to Hope: The Biography of Pope John Paul II.* New York: HarperCollins, 2005.

Weil, Simone. *Waiting for God.* London: Routledge Kegan Paul, 1951.

Wetzel, R. *Sexual Wisdom: A Guide for Parents, Young Adults, Educators and Physicians.* Huntington Beach, California: Sex Education for Advanced Beginners, 1998.

Williams, Rowan. "The Body's Grace," In *Theology and Sexuality.* Edited by Eugene F. Rogers, Jr. Oxford: Blackwells, 2002.

Zizek, Slavoj. *The Puppet and the Dwarf: The Perverse Core of Christianity.* Cambridge, Massachusetts: MIT Press, 2003.

Image Credits

Except for those otherwirse noted, all drawing and painting reproductions courtesy of the National Gallery of Art, Washington, DC.

Introduction

Chapter 1

Image Credits

Chapter 5

122 *St. Thomas Aquinas*, Italian, c. 1450, hand-colored woodcut.

129 *St. Thomas More*, Felix Bracquemond after Hans Holbein the Younger, French, 1883, etching.

139 *Jean-Jacques Rousseau*, Pierre-Michel Alix, French, 1803, color aquatint.

Chapter 6

144 *The Four Cardinal Virtues: Justice*, Netherlandish, sixteenth century, wool warp.

146 *Jacques Bénigne Bossuet*, Gerard Edelink, Flemish, c. 1700, etching and engraving.

150 *Allegorical Painting of Dante*, Italian, late sixteenth century, oil on panel.

165 Our Lady of Perpetual Help Chapel, Walsh University, Ohio, dedicated in 2009. Courtesy of Tyler Cosma and Terie Jusseaume.

Chapter 7

168 *The Presentation of the Lord*, Michael D. O'Brien, 1991. Courtesy of Michael D. O'Brien.

171 Corpus Christi procession, Oxford, United Kingdom. Author's collection.

177 Family bike ride in the country. Author's collection.

183 *The Alba Madonna*, Raphael, Italian, c. 1510, oil on panel.

187 A few students among the hundreds of thousands at the Washington, DC, March for Life. Courtesy of Thomas More College.

About the Author

A native of Saskatoon, Saskatchewan, Ryan N.S. Topping earned a doctorate in theology from the University of Oxford and is Fellow at Thomas More College of Liberal Arts in New Hampshire. He held the Pope John XXIII chair of studies in Catholic Theology at St. Thomas University in Canada. He is the author of St. *Augustine* (Continuum Press, 2010) and *Happiness and Wisdom: Augustine's Early Theology of Education* (Catholic University of American Press, 2011). He and his wife have five children.

Index

A

Allegorical Portrait of Petrarch, 41
Annunciation, Jan van Eyck, 208
Apollinarius, 60
Aquinas, St. Thomas, xx, 12, 24, 55, 58, 135, 152
Aristotle, 6, 135, 155–156, 164
Arius, 26, 61
Augustine, St., 8, 11, 16, 39, 40, 41, 76, 89, 91, 113, 135,
    145, 156, 164–166, 200, 213

B

Bacon, Francis, 202–204
Barth, Karl, 24
Baum, Gregory, 33–34
Beatrice, 152, 154
Benedict XVI, Pope, 22, 23, 34, 37, 46, 47, 72, 77, 78, 80, 86, 99,
    127, 170, 181, 201, 204, 205, 206, 217, 223, 229, 235, 238
Bible, xxi, 8, 16, 17, 18, 19, 20, 21, 22, 23, 24, 25, 158
Bolt, Robert, 128–130
Bouyer, Louis, 73, 238

C

Canadian Association of University Teachers (CAUT), 13
Caritas in Veritate, 52
Chaucer, Geoffrey, 9

Index

Index

An Invitation

Reader, the book that you hold in your hands was published by Sophia Institute Press.

Sophia Institute seeks to restore man's knowledge of eternal truth, including man's knowledge of his own nature, his relation to other persons, and his relation to God.

Our press fulfills this mission by offering translations, reprints, and new publications. We offer scholarly as well as popular publications; there are works of fiction along with books that draw from all the arts and sciences of our civilization. These books afford readers a rich source of the enduring wisdom of mankind.

Sophia Institute Press is the publishing arm of the Thomas More College of Liberal Arts and Holy Spirit College. Both colleges are dedicated to providing university-level education in the Western tradition under the guiding light of Catholic teaching.

If you know a young person who might be interested in the ideas found in this book, share it. If you know a young person seeking a college that takes seriously the adventure of learning and the quest for truth, bring our institutions to his attention.

www.SophiaInstitute.com
www.ThomasMoreCollege.edu
www.HolySpiritCollege.org

SOPHIA INSTITUTE PRESS

THE PUBLISHING DIVISION OF